A CRITIQUE OF
EUCHARISTIC AGREEMENT

D1292218

UNIFORM WITH THIS VOLUME

Modern Eucharistic Agreement (1973)   65p

Modern Ecumenical Documents on the Ministry (1975)   £1.50

A CRITIQUE
OF EUCHARISTIC
AGREEMENT

LONDON SPCK 1975

First published 1975
by S.P.C.K.
Holy Trinity Church
Marylebone Road
London NW1 4DU

© The Society for Promoting Christian Knowledge,1975

Printed in Great Britain by
Church Army Press, Cowley, Oxford

SBN 281 02820 6

CONTENTS

INTRODUCTION

John Lawrence

I have much fellow-feeling for the people referred to by the Bishop of Leicester in his contribution to this book 'who would never be impressed by a sermon on the Church as the Body of Christ but are capable of getting the right idea into their heads and hearts if Sunday after Sunday they say "We being many are one body, for we all partake of the one bread" '. I may live by the Holy Communion. I have certainly received much benefit from some books of eucharistic devotion. Eucharistic hymns are never far from the surface of my consciousness. But argument about the Holy Communion generally makes my mind go blank. I feel that 'they have taken away my Lord and I know not where they have put him'.

A layman invited to contribute to a book such as this cannot be expected to equal the technical competence of the experts who write in it, but he should know where the shoe pinches. How does such discussion come home to ordinary believers? Or does it pass them by? Obviously the contents of such books need some mediation before they can be absorbed by the ordinary man or woman in the pew, but the first book *Modern Eucharistic Agreement* and now these critical comments on it deal with things that do intimately concern every believer, however simple.

I am bound to say that, when I was reading this book, there were one or two moments when one or another contributor seemed to be beating the air, but these were exceptions. The matters treated are vital, the questions raised about them are inescapable. And they have been the subject of bitter controversy. So, to begin with, I ought to declare my own attitude to them in advance. I am not an adherent of any party in the Church of England. When Temple Gairdner of Cairo was asked whether he was High

Church or Low Church, he thought for a minute and then answered 'I hope I am deep Church'. I share that hope. If pressed further, I reply that I am a Catholic Evangelical.

This book is not an end in itself. It is part of a process which is either miraculous or fraudulent. In either case the process has a history that is, indeed, indicated in some of the contributions, and a future which may well contain surprises as great as those of the recent past.

Bishop Hanson writes that 'the title *Modern Eucharistic Agreement* is justified. An ecumenical consensus on the eucharist *has* been emerging. In some circles the appearance of the Anglican-Roman Catholic statement on the eucharist was greeted with the sceptical comment that those who produced it were simply anxious to produce agreement at any price. . . . But this book shows that such an interpretation is an impossible one. Indeed, no refutation of this attitude could have been more final than *Modern Eucharistic Agreement*. It is a stubborn and intransigent reminder that the Ecumenical Movement still exists, and indeed appears to be bearing fruit at the very moment when some have been proclaiming that it is declining'.

Dr Philip Edgecumbe Hughes thinks otherwise. He puts forward one of the traditional interpretations of the Holy Communion and quotes with approval Dr Francis Clark's judgement to the effect that 'it does not appear that the essentials of the problem have been changed. The new comprehensive language . . . may cover, but it does not resolve, the basic doctrinal tensions'. It should be explained that, apart from myself, none of the contributors to this volume saw in advance what the others were writing. No doubt this accounts for Dr Hughes's failure to give his answer to some of the objections that will undoubtedly be made against some of his views. But I find myself wondering whether there has been any meeting of minds between him and the other contributors on the points where they appear to differ. For instance, he writes that 'the notion that the sacrament invariably functions *ex opere operato*, as a means of grace to all who receive it, *without respect to the state of heart of the recipient*, must be set aside as erroneous'. But I was not aware that the words towards the end of the sentence which I have italicized were ever lawfully taught in any church. They would certainly be repudiated by the other contributors hereto. To say this is not in any way to refute the views of Dr Hughes, but rather to ask for a fuller exposition of them in the light of what the other contributors have written. As already pointed out, the discussion continues. And it should be emphasized that much of what Dr Hughes writes or quotes would be common ground.

He holds that 'eucharistic fellowship cannot be induced or contrived by the bureaucratic fiats of officialdom, which are more likely to smother than to promote it'. The Abbé Couturier would have agreed. Dr Hughes continues: 'Such fellowship must come about spontaneously, at the local level of worship. It will be the consequence not of ecumenical reports or of uniformitarian prescriptions, but of simple Christian open-heartedness which displays itself in open-table hospitality: the Lord's Table for the Lord's people.' Does this mean that if a Roman Catholic priest were to invite Dr Hughes to receive the Holy Communion at his hands, Dr Hughes would accept? And if not, why not? How much does eucharistic theology matter? Dr Hughes, if I have understood him, argues for the great importance of theological principle and then recommends a course of action which, on the face of it, leaves very little room for theological discernment. Obviously he has more to say, and I for one would like to hear it.

This brings us to something which I find missing in this and other similar discussions. We all agree that intercommunion, let alone a union of churches, must be based on a firm and clear agreement about essentials, but differing schools of thought give different lists of essentials, and so far as I can see, they do not tell us why these particular things and no others are essential. By what criterion should we in practice decide what agreement or doctrine is essential first for intercommunion and then for a union of churches? The section headed 'What do we mean by an "Agreement as to what is essential"?' on pp. 69–70 of *Modern Eucharistic Agreement* is interesting but it does not answer this. The problem is a general one, but it has a special application within the Anglican Church. All the contributors to this volume are Anglican priests. So presumably they are prepared to receive the sacrament from each other. Can any Anglican ask with integrity for a definition of essentials that is narrower than that which binds these very representative contributors together in spite of their disagreements?

Even if there is agreement on the principles of a criterion, to apply these principles will need patient ecumenical discussion. Supposing that all were agreed, for instance, that nothing may be required as essential that does not follow by direct implication from Scripture, experience makes it all too clear that there would be great difficulty in agreeing on what in fact does so follow, either in the field of eucharistic theology or any other field. All claim that their views are scriptural. I take it that Dr Hughes, and those who think like him, would in principle favour the joint examination of such matters by those who at present differ in their interpretation, on the principle, which he quotes with approval, that 'the ecumenical cause will be better served by frank scrutiny of the roots of disagreement than by ignoring them'. Readers will judge for themselves whether those who have entered into 'modern eucharistic agreements' have done precisely this, as most of the contributors to the present book appear to think, or whether, as Dr Hughes thinks, they have merely 'papered over the cracks'.

A third possibility is suggested by Bishop Hanson when he writes that 'an Anglican commentator may therefore, even though he is agreeably surprised at the consensus about the relation of the consecrated elements to Christ's body and blood, put a modest query against this consensus and ask whether anything valuable is gained by it, whether in the last analysis it has any particular meaning which is not better expressed in other ways'. Personally I would put this query more strongly, though I do in fact find that much of the language of these modern agreements is illuminating. All theological formulations must be constantly examined and re-examined in order to find out what, if anything, they mean and what other ways exist for expressing the truth they embody. But this brings us to the limits of human language. In the last resort we are all Nicodemuses. Human language is not adequate to express heavenly thought. Nor, indeed, is it to be expected that it would be.

If, as I hope, further volumes of this kind are to be published, I hope that some of them will speculate more boldly about the

4

relation between time and eternity, for the eucharist is the supreme event in our present experience when the eternal order overflows into the temporal order. Hence the difficulty, alluded to by several contributors, of saying anything at all about the location of Christ's presence in the Holy Communion. I do not underrate the difficulty of such an undertaking.

> Our knowledge of that life is small,
> The eye of faith is dim.

But we do know something and we ought to use the little that we know in order to learn more. Dr Mascall touches on this subject when he quotes Dom Anscar Vonier as maintaining that causality in the eucharist is of 'an entirely new type' and super-natural in a particular way. 'Sacraments are a new creation with entirely new laws.' I want to hear that argument developed.

I believe that a firm base has been laid for further advance and it is time to widen the scope of the inquiry in this and other respects. The search for eucharistic agreement is a search for eucharistic understanding. This should be universal for all mankind, but so far its consideration has been almost entirely European—and West European at that—and North American. It might not help to bring Asians and Africans into our private argument, but we should ask them to tell us what their own experience of the Holy Communion has been. I suspect that even more illumination would come from asking quite simple congregations to describe their experience, than from the professional theologians, though I can think of at least one Asian theologian whose views I would clearly like to hear. It is impossible to anticipate the answers, but it is virtually certain that they would move us to see our own understanding in a different light. If I am pressed to be more specific, I reply that it seems to me highly likely that a better understanding of that *participation intégrale*, which the West has lost almost completely but may now be beginning to recover, would cast new light on the theology of the Holy Communion.

It is only in a wider context, transcending not only the European tradition but also the limitations of our Newtonian or Einstinnian perceptions of time and space, that we could begin to develop Dr Mascall's pregnant hints about sacramental action as transfiguration. To prevent such inquiries becoming too rarified, I should like to see their results continually tested against the perceptions of ordinary congregations. Here I find myself in agreement with the Bishop of Truro in asking that these and other eucharistic agreements should be carefully checked with current traditional practice in worship, though I should expect these particular agreements—and modern eucharistic practice— to come rather better out of such an examination than the Bishop seems to anticipate. I like my theology to be congregational rather than individual, and perceptual before it is intellectual.

I thank God for the advances in ecumenical understanding made by theologians, but I am not altogether convinced by Bishop Hanson's contention that 'today theologians find it easier to agree than any other ecclesiastical group'. It depends on which theologians you ask and which other groups. The *lex orandi* is still the norm for the *lex credendi*. I am reminded of a remarkable sermon that I heard preached in the Cathedral of St Patrick at Armagh at a time when the North of Ireland was already being torn apart by the present communal strife, The argument was as follows: 'If you go into a Roman Catholic church you will find that the altar is the sole centre of attention. In a Presbyterian church you will find the pulpit where you expect to see the altar. In this church, since we are Anglicans, both the altar and the pulpit are given what we believe to be their due position. But if you go into any of these churches nowadays, and wait while the Holy Communion is celebrated, you can hardly fail to notice that the same thing is done, very often in almost the same words.' *Pace* Dr Hughes, the convergence appears unmistakable to most of those who have given their close attention to these phenomena.

As for the past, I cannot see that any of us here have been quite as consistent as we make out. But, so long as we are now in agreement, past dissension should no longer keep us apart. Bishop Hanson, writing from an Irish Protestant background not unlike my own, points out that 'the Anglican attitude has made its point. The Anglican protest, if protest it was, has been heard. This does . . . mean that there is no insuperable barrier between the Anglican communion and the Roman Catholic communion. No further point now remains in being Anglican for the sake of being Anglican'. He does not say that there is no barrier, but only no insuperable barrier. I would add that the same applies to the Eastern Orthodox Church and to the 'main line' Protestant Churches. Barriers there still are, but not insuperable barriers, and it is for us to overcome them.

AGREEMENTS:
THEIR SOURCES AND
FRONTIERS

R. R. Williams

There is little room in a symposium of this kind for an account of one's own spiritual odyssey or for detailed theological self-analysis. Much of my earlier life was passed among Evangelicals, particularly among the more liberal of them, but recent radical extremes both in doctrine and in biblical criticism have led me to make many friends among both Conservative Evangelicals and convinced Anglo-Catholics. I find much common ground with the seventeenth-century divines who, following on Richard Hooker, laid the foundations of the Anglicanism embodied in the Prayer Book of 1662. It is against this background that I articulate my reactions to the fascinating documents put together for us in the little book *Modern Eucharistic Agreement* (SPCK 1973).

It is clear to any thoughtful reader that the book reports and illustrates a remarkable consensus of opinion emerging in the 70s among many different ecclesiastical traditions, particularly on the nature of the eucharist.

Of most immediate interest to Anglicans is the first main document, the *Agreed Statement on Eucharistic Doctrine*, produced by the Anglican and Roman Catholic International Commission at Windsor in 1971 (after much preliminary work). Both the Anglican and Roman Catholic members of the Commission felt they had reached a substantial measure of agreement on eucharistic doctrine: on the nature of the mystery itself, on the eucharistic sacrifice, and on the real presence. Anyone familiar with the eucharistic controversies of the sixteenth, seventeenth,

9

eighteenth, and nineteenth centuries, will regard this as a very great event.

Then follows *A Lutheran-Roman Catholic Statement: the Eucharist as Sacrifice* (St Louis, Missouri, 1967). Again when one recalls the chasm that came to divide Luther from the main Roman Catholic Church in the sixteenth century, and how violently Luther reacted from the medieval doctrine of the mass as 'a propitiatory sacrifice for the living and the dead', one will be struck with wonder that such an agreement has proved possible.

Then comes the statement from the French group known as that of *Les Dombes*. This was a group primarily made up of French Reformed (i.e., Calvinistic) theologians, and French Roman Catholics. The group originated in the work of the Abbé Couturier, but, more recently, has been strongly influenced by the Taizé community. Its theological statement is largely based on that of the World Council (which concludes the book), but we are also given a 'commentary' and a 'pastoral agreement'. These reveal a strong 'social' content. The theological agreement is put into the context of the newer sense of political and social concern which is a prominent feature of Christian life and thought, particularly among the young, both in Europe and North America today. We note, especially, section VI of the doctrinal agreement (p. 66) 'The Eucharist: a Force for the Liberation of Mankind'.

By the action of the Spirit and the Ministry of the Church, Christ carries on the work for which he died and rose again: the work of freeing and reconciling all creation, in the first place by revealing to man the true face of God. When we accept his invitation to his table, we are taking up his mission in his footsteps by our witness of faith and hope, by our fight against the forces of oppression, destruction and death, in order to reconcile all things and offer everything to God . . . we cannot allow conditions to endure in which millions of men are deprived of bread, justice and peace.

The final statement in the book is the World Council statement, *The Eucharist in Ecumenical Thought*, produced in its final form at Louvain in 1971, but representing the fruit of a long series of conferences going back to Lund 1952.

The special importance of this statement is that it arose from a co-operative effort in which all the main confessional traditions were involved: Protestant, Anglican, Orthodox, and (to a limited degree) Roman Catholic. The Preamble contains a list of 'essential elements' in any true eucharist, and goes on to expound the eucharist under the headings 'The Lord's Supper', 'Thanksgiving to the Father', 'Memorial (*anamnesis*) of Christ', 'Mission to the World', 'End of Divisions'. All the *new* emphases are there: 'the Paschal Meal of the People of God'; the emphasis on the *epiclesis* (Eastern influence here?); the missionary aspect; and the dynamic understanding of eucharist as a means to unity, not only an expression of it.

With such a feast before us, it might seem churlish to 'ask for more'! It may, however, just be mentioned that the agreements we have here are by no means the only trans-confessional agreements of modern times. One might mention the *Arnoldshain Theses*. These were a series of eight theses agreed upon by Lutheran and Reformed scholars in Germany and first published in English in January 1959 in *The Ecumenical Review*. They attracted little attention at the time, and have not been formally accepted by the churches represented. But a glance at the wording shows that the dominant modern emphases are all there, e.g., Thesis I. 2:

In the communion the risen Lord invites his followers to his table, thus enabling them to participate here and now, in the future fellowship of the Kingdom of God.

Or again, Thesis IV:

The words which our Lord Jesus Christ speaks at the taking of the bread and the cup tell us what he himself gives in this meal to all who share in it. He, the crucified and risen Lord, allows himself, through his word of promise, to be taken in his body given in death for all, and his blood shed for all, and takes us by the strength of the Holy Spirit into the victory of his lordship by which we have forgiveness of sins, life and blessedness by faith in his promise.

The stress on eschatology and on dynamism is very marked.

11

B

More recently there has appeared in Bavaria the so-called *Leuenberg Concordat*. This again concerns Lutherans and Reformed, and it goes beyond the area of the eucharist. It is, however, providing an important talking-point in Lutheran circles. It gets a better reception in areas where there are strong Lutheran *and* Reformed elements; not so good a one where Lutherans are overwhelmingly predominant, as in Norway. It also produces a hostile reception in areas like Hungary, where the Lutherans are overshadowed by a large Roman Catholic and a large Reformed Church. When communities feel themselves very secure, or very threatened, they tend to rely on their existing defences.

In *Modern Eucharistic Agreement* we do not find reference to *Word and Sacrament* (SPCK 1968), the report of a representative conference of Anglican and German Evangelical theologians held in 1966 (exploratory, but very informative), nor to *Anglican-Lutheran International Conversations* (SPCK 1972), the report of the conversations held between the Anglican Communion (world-wide) and the Lutheran World Federation. In these conversations, which I had the privilege of chairing on the Anglican side, the eucharist did not figure largely. We had little difficulty in agreeing on a *short* statement; had we had to go into the subject more deeply, difficulties might have emerged.

It is interesting to note the dates of the documents in the recent book. They are (in order of appearance in the book) 1972, 1967, 1972, and 1971. They would appear to represent a growing consensus of opinion in many different lands and different churches during the later 60s and early 70s. In this connection I found it interesting to go back to a book of my own, *I believe—and why* (Mowbrays 1971), written in 1970. There, in a chapter on the Sacraments entitled 'One Baptism—one Bread', I described on pp. 80–84 the current mood of theological thought on several of the issues raised in this new book.

I draw attention to the chapters for this reason: I had not, when writing it, read any of the documents printed in *Modern Eucharistic Agreement* (indeed they were mostly not completed), but the similarity between what I was saying and what runs through these agreements is now very clear to me. I could not

12

easily say by what authority I said those things! They represented my view of the theological climate, and just because they were undocumented, they indicate the prevailing wind of which all sensitive observers could not fail to be aware.

THE ESSENCE OF THE AGREEMENTS

Although the strong similarity between the outlook of the various statements produced in *Modern Eucharistic Agreement* is plain to any thoughtful reader, it may be worth while for a contributor to this book of comments on the statements to give his own summary of the salient points of agreement as they strike him. Prominent among the points of agreement is a common belief in 'the mystery of the Eucharist'. Thus the Anglican and Roman Catholic *Agreed Statement* (*M.E.A.*, p. 26) says:

> Christ through the Holy Spirit in the eucharist builds up the life of the Church, strengthens its fellowship and furthers its mission.

The same point is emphasized strongly in the Doctrinal Agreement produced by the group at Les Dombes. See, for example, the Statement on p. 57:

> The eucharist is the sacramental meal, the new paschal meal of God's people, which Christ, having loved his disciples unto the end, gave them before his death that they might celebrate it in the light of the resurrection until his coming.

Similar statements can be found in all the Agreements.

The importance of this common starting point lies in the fact that no longer is the holy sacrament thought of primarily as a means of grace for the individual communicant. Of course it *is* this. The individual communicant continues to benefit from all that Christ has to give in the sacrament. There is a difference, however, between 'coming to communion' and being part of the communion fellowship. Moreover, what is going on is not just a club meal, although Pliny in the early part of the second century, in describing the sacrament to Trajan, brought the whole activity under the heading of club life, something that had been forbidden

13

by Trajan. It is natural enough for the external observer to see things in this way. To the Christian mind, however, it is much more than this. Every celebration of the communion is linked to all those that have gone before since 'the night in which he was betrayed', and with all those that will take place 'until he comes'. Although each communion service is specially limited to one point on the earth's surface, it is well known that hundreds of other celebrations are going on, either at the same time or immediately before and after the particular one in question. Besides this historical and geographical 'spread', every holy communion has a spiritual or a supernatural dimension. Just as Christ was the host at the original supper, gave the gifts of bread and wine, and commanded his disciples 'to do this in remembrance of' him, so still he is the host and all is done at his command.

The meal is rightly described as a *paschal* meal, for each communion is closely linked with the Easter victory which was itself the culmination of the Easter sacrifice. Were it not for the fact that custom of the primitive Church linked the eucharist with the Lord's Day ('And upon the first day of the week, when we were gathered together to break bread' Acts 20. 7), we might well have imagined that the Christian eucharist was intended to be a new Passover, celebrated once a year. It is perhaps not altogether a coincidence that the special prominence given to the Easter communion in our Anglican tradition, and indeed in the whole tradition of Christendom, expresses something of this paschal note. Not for nothing do we sing at Eastertime, 'Christ our Passover is sacrificed for us'. Not for nothing do we say in the special preface for Easter, 'For he is our very paschal lamb'. However, just as every Lord's Day has something in it of the atmosphere of the first Easter Day, so every celebration of the communion has something of the atmosphere of the paschal celebration.

The mere fact that all the great Christian traditions now approach the eucharist with this strong biblical and 'Primitive Church' background, is itself something that separates the modern eucharistic agreement from the individual traditions that developed in isolation from each other during the earlier history of the Church, e.g., the Eastern separated from the Western; the

14

Reformation separated from the Roman; the Lutheran separated from the Calvinist; and so on.

All this is expressed in the important sentence given prominence in the Anglican Series II service: 'We being many are one body, for we all partake of the one bread'. There may indeed be certain dangers in this almost exclusive attention to the eucharist as the source and origin of the corporate nature of the Church (how about Baptism?), but at the moment we can be thankful for the emphasis that has been put upon it and for the wide measure of agreement which it has conjured up.

The next item on which there is a large measure of agreement is the doctrine of the eucharistic sacrifice. In all these statements there is a balance struck between two equally important facts. The first is that the sacrifice of Christ upon Calvary (what Protestants used to call the finished work) was a once-for-all achievement, never to be repeated. This goes right against the medieval Roman Catholic tradition of the mass as a regular propitiatory sacrifice for the living and the dead, as was finally stated at the Council of Trent. On the other hand it is agreed that sacrifice, and thoughts of sacrifice, cannot be excluded even in the most biblically based view of the holy communion. It is agreed on all sides that there is a sacrifice of praise and thanksgiving, and an offering of ourselves either with or as a response to the sacrifice of Christ on our behalf. It is, however, now agreed, even by the Lutherans and the Calvinists, that there is something more sacrificial in the whole event of the communion than has usually been recognized. The way in which this bridge is produced over the chasm between Catholic sacrificialists and Reformed non-sacrificialists is by means of the new understanding of memorial (*anamnesis*). Broadly speaking, all the contributors to these new agreed statements accept the view of *anamnesis* popularized by such continental theologians as Dahl and Jeremias. The first time I myself became familiar with this view was when many years ago I read for the first time *Die Abendmahlsworte Jesu* by Dr J. Jeremias (2nd edn, Zwingli-Verlag, Zurich 1949; E. T., *The Eucharistic Words of Jesus*, SCM Press, 1955). It was then that I came to believe that the words 'in remembrance of me' really should be translated 'for a memorial of me'; a memorial, that is, in God's sight. I was very struck by Jeremias's reference (op. cit., p. 117) where the author compares the eucharistic words of Jesus with the words in Acts 10. 4: 'Thy prayers are gone up as a memorial before God'. With this interpretation of *anamnesis* goes the further point that the Passover was more than just a way of reminding people of a past event. It brought them under the influence of the past event in such a way that the past event became present. It is in this sense that the eucharist is seen to have a sacrificial dimension. Without saying that the sacrifice is repeated, it is in some way made present and contemporary, and the worshippers are caught up into the sacrificial act.

It must not be assumed that everybody is ready to accept this interpretation of memorial. Thus R. T. Beckwith in *The Churchman* (Spring 1973), quotes the statement from the Catholic Information Office on the *Agreed Statement* saying that 'Christ established the memorial to make present and real his historic sacrifice each time the eucharist is celebrated'. Beckwith rejects the 'making present' theory and stresses the fact that the memorial was concerned with 'reminding and remembering', as certain passages in the Old Testament demonstrate to his satisfaction. He thinks that this new theory is based upon a comparison between eucharist and the rites of the mystery religions. I do not personally take this view. I am satisfied with the Old Testament and related quotations brought to the fore by Jeremias, and do indeed think that the Passover was a making present of the Passover events with all their consequences. In this sense for many years I have had no difficulty in using sacrificial language in connection with the eucharist, although, having been born and brought up an Evangelical, I always feel that I must guard myself against treating the eucharist as a direct sequel to the sacrificial cults of the Old Testament. The words of the hymn:

> Finished all the types and shadows
> Of the ceremonial law

represent something deep in my blood, but I do not think that this prevents me from feeling the atmosphere of sacrifice surrounding the eucharist. However Protestant one may be at heart, there is still the picture in our minds of the Lamb before the throne representing us as one who died and rose again, and ever lives to make intercession for us.

The third great subject in which agreement is notified is a common understanding of the presence of Christ in the sacrament. A typical sentence comes from the Agreed Statement between the Anglicans and Roman Catholics: 'Communion with Christ in the eucharist presupposes his true presence effectually signified by the bread and wine which, in this mystery, become his body and blood'. Or again, 'The elements are not mere signs; Christ's body and blood become really present and are really given. But they are really present and given in order that receiving them, believers may be united in communion with Christ the Lord'. (*M.E.A.*, pp. 28–9)

Throughout all the statements the balance is struck in this way. Great stress is laid on what one might call the general presence of Christ with his people in accordance with his promise, 'Where two or three are gathered together in my name there am I in the midst'. Further thoughts about presence are to be taken in that context. However, great stress is also laid on the fact that his Word and promise are as true today as they were when first uttered. 'This *is* my body and this *is* my blood.' What finally emerges is something very different from anything like transubstantiation (a subject reduced to a small footnote in the Anglican-Roman Catholic *Agreed Statement*) and it is not particularly like what one might call the Anglo-Catholic substitute for transubstantiation. Nor is it very much like the Lutheran doctrine of consubstantiation. The agreement rests on an assurance that Christ himself is really present and that the words of consecration (to use a now old-fashioned form of expression) are still divinely authorized and spiritually valid. To be quite honest, what finally comes out is very much like what used to be written and expounded by the classical Anglican divines of the seventeenth century, particularly by Bishop Andrewes. These similarities are brought out in the introductory notes by the Bishop of Ossory, Dr McAdoo, who is himself, of course, a leading authority on classical Anglicanism.

It is not really surprising that there is a similarity. Our Anglican divines in that century were reacting to their medieval inheritance, cross-bred, to to speak, with the biblical emphases of the Reformation. They therefore stressed the reality of the gift (This is my body) with an assertion that we do not know *in what way* these words are to be defined and interpreted. They stressed both the positive and the negative side of truth as they saw it, the certainty of the gift and our ignorance as to the method. In modern times we have a coming together of Roman Catholics and those whose minds have been formed by three centuries of Reformation insights. It is not surprising that the final result is something very much like Anglican synthesis of the seventeenth century.

It may be profitable now to ask ourselves how it is that these agreements have proved possible after so many years and centuries of division. I think we can detect three principal sources of the new spirit. First there is the great increase in mutual knowledge. There are many sources whereby this knowledge has been increased. One can think of the visits from two Archbishops of Canterbury to two successive Popes; of the Protestant observers at Vatican II; of the Roman Catholic observers at World Council meetings, both in Geneva and in many other countries. Travel is easier than it has ever been in the past, and mutual tolerance makes it possible for men to talk and exchange experience in a relaxed atmosphere. The underlying common ground is at last revealed when the top strata of misunderstanding through historical isolation have been cleared away. We should, I think, go further and say that the Holy Spirit has been at work in producing true love and understanding in many of these meetings, which could so easily have been confrontations, and have instead proved to be great episodes of reconciliation.

It is probably true that had not the varying parties in these consultations wished to come to an agreement, they never would have done so. It is because their love made it impossible for them to remain separated in heart and mind that they went on until they could express agreement, at least over a large area of eucharistic doctrine.

Another source of agreement is to be found in the progress which has been made in biblical criticism. There is a very great difference between the present attitude of scholars, both Catholic and non-Catholic, to the Scriptures, compared with that which prevailed fifty or a hundred years ago. The human element in all Scripture is recognized and among scholars in all traditions the scriptural writings are seen, as it were, in perspective rather than on one flat level. The material to be considered by New Testament scholars when considering the eucharist is to be found first of all in 1 Corinthians and then in the Synoptic Gospels, within which there are certain important differences, particularly as between Mark and Luke. There is the theological material to be found in the Fourth Gospel, which has a direct bearing on eucharistic teaching, and there is all the new knowledge whereby Old Testament and rabbinical thought has been made to contribute to the understanding of eucharistic teaching in the New Testament. Those who take a strongly fundamental or literalist view of the Scriptures are few and far between, whether one goes to Rome, Geneva, Canterbury, or New York. The fact that scholars of all traditions are approaching the biblical material with the same criteria in mind is a potent source of a new attitude to divergent traditions. All can be judged alike by the same criteria, for different degrees of distortion have crept in through centuries of exegesis based on what are now known to be inadequate foundations.

A third source of agreement is to be found in the changing perspective which affects the attitude of Christians of all traditions in the modern world. In days gone by, all within Christendom accepted the basic tenets of the Christian Creeds and read the Scriptures in the light of them. This meant that differences about details loomed much larger than they do today. In the modern world belief in God is at a discount, and there are many varieties of belief in Jesus Christ, not all of which are soundly based on the Chalcedonian definition. Whereas in the past Christians quarrelled violently about Christology (in the fourth and fifth centuries) and about the eucharist (in the fifteenth and sixteenth centuries), all alike now face a challenge to the fundamental theistic assumptions on which Christian faith has to be based. When it is necessary to contend earnestly for belief in God, for faith in Christ and for some firm grasp on an eternal world it is no time for Christians to be quarrelling about the *minutiae* of the interpretation of one of the two sacraments. These considerations do not undermine the value of the new agreements, but it is helpful to keep them in mind so that the proportion of faith in our modern world may be properly understood.

SOME REMAINING QUESTIONS

It is no good pretending that all questions have already been solved. I mention a few outstanding issues which are either left in abeyance in these documents, or are in some way glossed over.

First there is the question of the minister. Does it matter who celebrates the holy communion? It is customary to say today that the whole congregation celebrates. However, as this question is dealt with in the publication, *Modern Ecumenical Documents on the Ministry*, I shall not discuss it in detail here. If I were to give my own personal view of this matter, I should say that there is infinite value in the apostolic succession and that the Church will always need a ministry thus rooted in history and in the will and purpose of our Lord.

Another question is, how far these formal statements really express the attitude of ordinary church people in the different traditions. A good example of the difference between official and popular attitudes occurred in 1965 at the four-hundred-and-fiftieth anniversary of the nailing of Luther's theses. I and other Anglicans attending Sunday morning service in a village near Wittenberg decided to 'stay on' to receive holy communion, to show solidarity with the suffering Christians of East Germany. To our surprise and embarrassment, about 95 per cent of the congregation of about four hundred departed, leaving us not quite sure as to how we should conduct ourselves. No doubt this kind of experience could be repeated in many parts of the world.

A third question which I should like to pose is a more difficult and far-reaching one. It really goes to the root of a great many controversies which have divided the Church down the centuries, and perhaps it is not too much to say that one can see the roots of it even in the New Testament itself in different statements in the First Epistle to the Corinthians, not entirely harmonious the one with the other, and still more clearly in the Fourth Gospel where, in 6. 53, 63, one can see material on which both the

Catholic and the Protestant traditions about the presence of Christ in the eucharist have been and indeed still are based. The question is whether the idea of presence should ever have been tied up with the words of consecration, as we commonly call them, 'This is my body, and this is my blood'. Clearly there is some symbolism in the language, but there is also realism. Perhaps we could say that the symbolism is realistic, and the realism is symbolic. All the discussions that have gone on about the relation between the outward and the inward gift are logical and appropriate. They flow naturally from the situation created by the words of our Lord at the Last Supper, and by their use in sacramental worship ever since. It was, I believe, Latimer who first related the idea of presence to the promised gift of the body and the blood, and subsequently this came right into the heart of Anglican discussion and controversy about the presence. It was well and truly launched in the so-called 'Black Rubric' of the 1552 Prayer Book which, while allowing kneeling, insisted that there was no 'real and essential' presence intended. The rubric as a whole was reprinted in the 1662 Prayer Book, but with the word 'corporal' inserted (as rejected) instead of 'real and essential'. This left by implication 'real and essential' presence closely related to the elements as the whole matter was being discussed under the heading 'On kneeling to receive the sacrament'. I am inclined to think that however realistically one may take the sacramental gifts to convey what our Lord intended them to convey, namely his body and blood, it might have been better if the word 'presence' had been kept in a separate category for his spiritual presence with his people, promised at all times, promised particularly at their worship, and undoubtedly realized at all times and in all places in a very special way in the eucharistic sacrament.

The final question I should like to pose is how far liturgy reflects doctrine, or alternatively, how far doctrine is moulded by liturgy. This is particularly important at the present time. The situation may vary from country to country, but I hazard the view that the English people are, of all peoples, the least theologically minded. Abstract ideas count for little in the thought of English people, whether in politics or in theology. Their minds and their outlook are moulded by things that happen. It is true that

behind the Reformation Prayer Book there was a new understanding of the Pauline doctrine of justification by faith, and a
new emphasis on the full, perfect and sufficient sacrifice of Christ
upon the cross. This undoubtedly is reflected in the classical
English Prayer Books. Being there strongly and clearly presented, being heard and spoken of, year after year, century after
century, some of the ideas came to have a rooted place in the
thought and outlook of the people. This would mean that the
deliberate contradiction of ideas that have been worked into
people's minds by long liturgical use would create for them
questions and problems. We now have services, like Series II,
where the whole emphasis, or a great deal of it, is on the contemporary building-up of the Body of Christ, the Church, through
mutual fellowship and through the sharing in the divine gift.
People who would never be impressed by a sermon on 'the
Church as the body of Christ' are capable of getting the idea right
into their heads and hearts if Sunday after Sunday they say
'We being many are one body, for we all partake of the one
bread'.

This then raises the enormously important subject as to
whether the communion should be thought of primarily in hori-
zontal or in vertical dimension. By this I mean, is the whole
stress to be upon the contemporary here-and-now fellowship of
Christians, going out into here-and-now service of their fellow-
men, or alternatively, is it to be a gift from above, a communion
with God through the crucified, risen and ascended Christ, and a
thankful remembrance for his atoning death? As is brought out
by an article by John Riches in *Theology* for April 1974, Fellowship and service seem to conflict with remembrance, worship,
and a supernatural gift. Carried to its extreme form (as Professor
Willi Marxsen expressed in a Conference I attended in 1966) the
contemporary interpretation leads towards a Quaker approach,
i.e., that every meal is a sacrament. The transcendental, vertical
dimension tends towards a service set apart from other activities
by consecrated buildings, special vestments, solemn spiritual
preparation. It may be necessary for us to incorporate the contemporary without losing our grasp on the transcendental. Laud
had to put the altars back again to the East wall of the churches,

to ensure reverence and a sense of mystery. We are now in a strong '1552' atmosphere ('table in the body of the church'). How soon shall we need, and find, a new Laud?

EUCHARISTIC AGREEMENT: AN ECUMENICAL AND THEOLOGICAL CONSENSUS

R. P. C. Hanson

The four statements about eucharistic doctrine published in *Modern Eucharistic Agreement* have very different origins. The Anglican-Roman Catholic International Commission produced its statement after several years' joint discussion held in regular meetings lasting several days by experts in the subjects covered. Its authority is carefully defined by Dr McAdoo in his Introduction. It is not an official statement representing the formal views of both churches. But it does represent expert opinion. Its authority is academic, not official, but to many this is a weighty authority, more weighty, perhaps, than an official one might be. The Lutheran-Roman Catholic statement is the product of three meetings lasting three days each during the year 1967, and therefore must lack something of the authority possessed by the first group because it represents a shorter period of deliberation. The third statement from the Group of Les Dombes resulted from the meeting over a much longer period than the others of a consciously like-minded group composed of French Roman Catholics and French Protestants, who were concerned with the implications of their agreement for a much wider area of Christian thought than that with which the other groups were concerned. The fourth statement emanates from a Commission of the World Council of Churches, and is an attempt to describe and evaluate 'the emerging ecumenical consensus' on the eucharist. Its authors (anonymous in this publication) must have comprised a much wider denominational compass than did any of the other groups. It is perhaps worth noting that Anglicans figured prominently in the membership of only one of these groups.

Yet the agreement which all four groups reached independently of each other is remarkable. The title *Modern Eucharistic Agreement* is justified. An ecumenical consensus on the eucharist *has* been emerging. In some circles the appearance of the Anglican-Roman Catholic *Agreed Statement* on the eucharist was greeted with the sceptical comment that those who produced it were simply anxious to achieve agreement at any price, to paper over the cracks in order to produce an appearance of harmony. But this book shows that such an interpretation is an impossible one. Indeed, no refutation of this attitude could have been more final than this book. The Roman Catholics and Anglicans were, we now realize, only some of a number of Christians of diverse traditions who are finding it possible to reach substantial agreement on the eucharist. These statements cannot be dismissed as insignificant. They support each other in a most surprising way. It is easy to understand that this agreement which seems possible to so many different groups in different parts of the world might cause alarm and despondency among other groups in other parts. All those who have a vested interest in controversy between Christians (and there are thousands of Christians who have such an interest, acknowledged or not); all Protestants challenged to change their minds about Roman Catholics; all Catholics who are disturbed at the thought that Protestants might after all have been believing Catholic doctrine about the eucharist; all those who are floating with the current of anti-ecumenical sentiment which is to be noted in several places today, will find this book a difficult fact to explain away. It is a stubborn and intransigent reminder that the Ecumenical Movement still exists, and indeed appears to be bearing fruit at the very moment when some have been proclaiming that it is declining. The conspiracy theory will not stand up to the evidence produced here, either. The conspiracy theory has two forms: either the crafty Roman Catholics are luring the unwary Protestants into a trap by pretending friendship and readiness to find common ground with them, but in reality in order to swallow them whole; or a number of cynical prelates of different denominations are keeping the Ecumenical Movement

26

going in order that they may enjoy the delights of foreign cooking, foreign travel, and sight-seeing (in the intervals of attending Conferences) at the expense of their denominations. This little book makes it clear that ecumenical understanding and the seeking of common ground are neither a conspiracy nor a racket. They are the concern and the creation of honest, single-hearted and well-informed Christians.

The actual doctrinal agreement reached is impressive, and it has been reached in a way which is daring and honest rather than evasive and circumlocutory; the Les Dombes statement even points out that such an agreement has made severe demands upon both traditions in the dialogue and that controversial points have not been avoided. All the statements agree that the body and blood of Christ are really given in the eucharistic sacrament, that they are received by the faithful believer but are present in some sense independently of his faith. This might be regarded as a series of Protestant concessions, but of course this would be a crude way of looking at the matter, because these doctrines are in fact part of the tradition of almost all the non-Roman Catholic groups represented in these statements. On the other hand, in one statement (the Anglican-Roman Catholic *Agreed Statement*) the doctrine of transubstantiation is relegated to a footnote with the explanation that this doctrine affirms the fact of Christ's presence but does not explain how the change in the elements takes place. And in the Lutheran-Roman Catholic statement 'a spatial or natural manner of presence' is explicitly rejected. In the Les Dombes statement it is denied that Christ is localized in the bread and wine or that they undergo any physico-chemical change. These might by short-sighted persons be regarded as concessions by the Roman Catholics, were it not that they are not difficult to reconcile with Catholic doctrine. I remember some years ago in conversation with a dear friend of mine, a Roman Catholic priest now departed this life, who could not be described as an advocate of radical or advanced theology, hearing him remark almost casually that Catholics of course believed that Christ was present in the eucharist in a spiritual manner. When the Church of Ireland, frightened by what appeared to it to be the excesses of Anglo-Catholicism, added a clause to its catechism

27

declaring that Christ was present in the sacrament of holy communion 'only after a heavenly and spiritual manner', it was not denying Catholic doctrine but affirming it.

The *Agreed Statement* (*M.E.A.*, p. 28) says that the bread and wine became Christ's body and blood. The American Lutheran-Roman Catholic statement (*M.E.A.*, p. 40) says that in the sacrament Jesus Christ is present wholly and entirely in his body and blood. The Les Dombes statement (*M.E.A.*, pp. 59–60) affirms that the reality given in the signs of the bread and wine is Christ's body and blood. (The statement of the WCC Commission lacks any statement corresponding to these.) Once again, the agreement is striking, but we may well ask, what do these statements mean? We do not intend to raise the old controversies which distracted the men of the sixteenth and subsequent centuries; we do not intend to throw around accusations of idolatry. But in the light of studies by scholars of many different traditions over the last twenty or thirty years in the nature of biblical language and of language generally, we are bound to ask what, more exactly, does it mean to say that the bread and the wine in the eucharist are or become Christ's body and blood? Are we to take this state literally and to conclude that, as Christ rose from the dead unchanged in his physical substance, so we now, when we communicate in the eucharist, somehow receive or encounter this physical substance? Quite apart from the many other objections raised by such a theory, it would flatly contradict St Paul's doctrine of Christ's resurrection. Whatever other obscurities may attach to this doctrine, it is quite clear that for Paul, Christ did not rise from the dead unchanged. On the contrary, he rose a spiritual body, and flesh and blood cannot inherit the Kingdom of God. Again, the whole tradition of Hebraic thought suggests that words such as 'body' and 'blood' used in solemn religious formulae are most unlikely to be literal and no more than literal in their meaning, any more than they are likely to be purely arbitrary symbols. Biblical language lends itself neither to the medieval tendency to turn images into metaphysics nor into the literalist desire to take them as scientific statements. In speaking of Christ's body and blood as present in the eucharist we are using the highly symbolic, highly equivocal language of imagery, and it is only a matter of common sense to tread carefully and delicately here; we are taking one further step into semantic complexity when we say that the consecrated bread and wine are or become Christ's body and blood. It is even doubtful whether this can be described as formal Anglican doctrine. Of course it must not be thought to be contrary to Anglican doctrine, and for some considerable time now many Anglicans have believed this doctrine in some sense. But on the whole it has been the Anglican tradition not to take this further step, i.e., not to say that the bread and wine are not Christ's body and blood, but not to say that they are. The Anglican doctrine upon this subject since the end of the sixteenth century at latest has consistently been that the consecrated elements convey, are the vehicles of, Christ's body and blood, in such a way that he who partakes in faith receives Christ's body and blood and he who does not partake or does not partake in faith does not thus sacramentally receive Christ's body and blood. And if challenged further as to what receiving Christ's body and blood means, the great majority of Anglican theologians and of Anglican communicants would say that it means being made sharers in Christ's life. With this conviction goes a host of allied beliefs: that we are made sharers of Christ's self-giving, of his sufferings, of his victory, of his redemption, that his vicarious sacrifice is here applied to us, and so on. An Anglican commentator may therefore, even though he is agreeably surprised at the consensus about the relation of the consecrated elements to Christ's body and blood, put a modest query against this consensus, and ask whether anything valuable is gained by it, whether in the last analysis it has any particular meaning which is not better expressed in other ways.

This query will be all the sharper because in virtually every other respect these four statements agree in taking an approach to the eucharist, which is not contradictory to, but not manifestly consonant with, the queried doctrine. The eucharistic doctrine of all four statements (and not least of the *Agreed Statement*) is dynamic. It sees the eucharist in terms of movement, of act, of drama. In this sacrament Christ gives himself, we offer ourselves. The whole rite is a dialogue or encounter, an event. It is the out-going of God in Christ to his people, and the return of his people

29

to him through Christ. The Les Dombes statement particularly emphasizes that the sacrament is only effective and the occasion significant because it is done in the Holy Spirit. (It is interesting to observe that its emphasis upon the necessity of the *epiclesis*, which is liturgically indefensible, is corrected in the WCC statement.) The Church calls upon the Holy Spirit and he in response brings them into union with Christ through communion in the bread and the wine. All the various traditional elements of the eucharist, memorial and sacrifice and communion, are caught up into a conception of the eucharist as movement. The thought stirs in all four statements like a restless wind. This is of course the result of the kind of theology which most of us have been used to for the past thirty years, whether one recalls the dynamism which is so strong a feature of Karl Barth's dogmatic thought, or the theories of the exponents of process theology, or the findings (still not entirely obsolete or disproved) of the biblical scholars who have, in this dynamic character, seen one of the chief ways in which Hebraic thought differs from Greek. It should be obvious how ill such an emphasis consorts with the apparently static or undynamic doctrine that the consecrated bread and wine *are* the body and blood of Christ.

The Anglican-Roman Catholic *Agreed Statement* is the shortest and makes no attempt to link agreement on the eucharist with agreement on any other field of doctrine. In fact the same commission which produced this statement has since gone on to consider the doctrine of ministry. The Lutheran-Roman Catholic statement notes that it has said nothing about ministry. But the last two statements, that of Les Dombes and that of the WCC Commission, go out of their way to note that agreement on the eucharist implies and demands agreement on other subjects too, and cannot be left by itself. A number of related topics are raised as soon as it is realized that substantial agreement on the eucharist can be achieved: apostolicity, ministry, continuity and, behind all these, authority, must now logically come up for consideration. Christian doctrine, like peace, is indivisible. This book opens to us a large vista of possibility. If bodies as opposed and contrary as Roman Catholics, Lutherans, French Protestants, and Anglicans have conventionally been can agree upon a subject as controversial as the eucharist, it is not difficult to envisage the area of agreement becoming wider and wider.

It could well be imagined that an agreement on doctrine as comprehensive as this agreement might be, with all the far-reaching consequences which it would bring with it, is likely to bring bewilderment to the ordinary observer. How is it that these agreements have been possible, so suddenly, all within the space of two years? What has happened? It cannot be a trick or an hallucination. It cannot be a carefully devised façade. The answer lies partly in the fact that the theologians in the different denominations have discovered a new way of conducting ecumenical dialogue. Untill recently the method used for ecumenical dialogue had been that of the World Council of Churches, i.e., the gathering together of a large number of theologians representing almost the whole spectrum of denominations into populous conferences at relatively long intervals. The result was a lack of continuity, an inevitable impression of incoherence and the suggestion of a Lowest Common Denominator theology; it also meant that the Conferences tended to be dominated by one or two major theologians (usually German). Something of these defects can still be seen attaching to the WCC statement in this book. But the other statements resulted from the meeting of relatively small numbers of theologians at relatively short intervals, not open to domination by star performers, working in private and not in the journalistic limelight which appears to be inseparable from the major activities of the World Council of Churches. And there was almost complete continuity in each group. This method of what might be called bi-denominational discussion has produced remarkable results in the first three statements and is well worth studying. A great deal of credit must, of course, be given to the Ecumenical Movement even though none of the first three groups may have arisen directly out of its inspiration. It obviously had prepared the ground (no less obviously than had the Second Vatican Council), and can indeed even be said to have given a paradigm of the bi-denominational discussion in the consultations between the Eastern Orthodox and Oriental Orthodox theologians which met under its auspices in Aarhus in 1964 and in Bristol in 1967, with such remarkable results.

The other, and even more powerful, cause of this surprising agreement between theologians of such diverse backgrounds is that all have been influenced by the current of theological thought and the development of theological scholarship which have taken place during the last half century. There has been an extraordinary loosening of old allegiances and severing of old loyalties and disappearance of old barriers. The development of historical criticism, the Liturgical Movement which so strangely over-leaped the boundaries of denomination, the Second Vatican Council with all that flowed from it, the emergence of a kind of Scholars' International whereby theologians read each other's works, met each other, exchanged ideas and papers, and all in common contributed, and felt that they were contributing, to a single ongoing discipline, to the same enterprise of free explora-tion expressed in study and scholarship, created an unpre-cedented atmosphere of theological change, theological enterprise, theological cross-fertilization. It is this, more than anything else, that has made these agreements possible. It is noteworthy too that—as the first of these statements explicitly says—the framers of these statements have tried to go behind the stereotyped formulae and controversy-stamped ideas of the sixteenth and seventeenth centuries, and even of the Middle Ages, in order to concentrate upon the thought concerning the eucharist of the New Testament, the early Fathers and the early liturgies. That is why they are for the most part devoid of technical terms and conventional theological phrases. Experts in eucharistic theology, or at least in the history of eucharistic theology, will miss the old familiar battle-cries and passwords. Accidents, substance, virtu-alism, oblation, reservation, extra-liturgical devotions, prayer of consecration, 'in, with and under', consubstantiation, corrupt following of the apostles, offering Christ for the quick and the dead, adoration of the corporal presence of Christ—they have mostly been swept away as words which belong to a limbo or dustbin of history. The theological revolution which has shaken the very basis of Christianity during the last two centuries, and whose existence has now at last been recognized by all the major denominations of the West, has at least had this healthy result: it has shaken the theologians out of the grooves in which their thought previously ran and enabled them to climb over the old trenches, leave their strongly entrenched positions, and shake hands with each other in the open.

But it is to be noted that this is an agreement of theologians. In the case of the Les Dombes group we can add that a spiritual and moral concern was present along with an intellectual and theological one, and this group drew out the practical and pastoral implications of their agreement at some length. But those who came to these remarkable agreements were primarily interested in theology, and most of them were clergy (in the case of the first group, all were clergy, and for all one can tell, in the case of the second group also). It is a surprising but incontestable fact that today the theologians find it easier to agree than any other ecclesiastical group. It was not, for instance, the theologians who were responsible for the collapse of the Anglican-Methodist unity scheme. The trouble in that situation was not too much theology but too little. A century ago it was generally assumed that in any attempt of divided Christian bodies to come closer to each other the difficulties and obstacles would be provided by the theologians, whereas the ordinary rank-and-file would not find it difficult to understand each other. But today the theologians are far ahead of the main body of believers in every denomination when it comes to agreement in doctrine. Theologians do not have the reputation of being soft-headed sentimentalists. It is not sentimentalism that has brought them together, but the honest following of their own theological assumptions and convictions and methods. Unlike other Christians, they know too much to be divided by anything less than the truth. The fact is that theology today can only be done satisfactorily on an ecumenical basis. The crisis in which the Christian faith finds itself today ignores denominational barriers, applies indiscriminately to all Christians, and can be met adequately only by all the intellectual and spiritual resources available in every Christian tradition that commands the allegiance of men and women of honesty and goodwill. Doing theology on a denominational basis is wantonly restricting the truth, trying to bound the Holy Spirit in a nutshell. The day of denominational theology is past. The old shibboleths grow faint, the old slogans no longer attract, except perhaps in Northern

Ireland; and Northern Ireland is a ghastly example of what happens if denominationalism is allowed to become a permanent feature in society; men begin by defending church principles and end by child murder.

But in this 'emerging ecumenical consensus', which covers not only those points where ecumenical consensus used to be thought least likely, but a great deal of the rest of Christian doctrine as well, there is no reason why Anglicanism should be submerged. On the contrary, instead of being submerged it will be fulfilled. Of course, if Anglicanism is defined (as it tends to be in some parts of the Anglican Communion) with a stark simplicity as 'that which is not Roman Catholic', then there can, by definition, be no agreement at all, just as if Lutheranism sees its main *raison d'être* as witnessing against the Church of Rome, then nothing further can be said. When I was a curate in Dublin thirty years ago, some of the older clergy used to dream of a millenium in which the Irish people would see the error of their ways and abandon the Church of Rome and turn in their thousands to the Church of Ireland. These clergy had not the least idea about how this could come about and made no serious effort at all to prepare their church for this eschatological event. Thirty years later, as an Irish bishop, I tried to persuade my fellow-clergy that something very like this millenium was taking place, not that the Irish Roman Catholics were flocking into the Church of Ireland, but that the Church of Rome was reforming its doctrine in a direction which looked suspiciously like an Anglican one. Where I was not met by blank refusal to believe, I usually encountered alarm and perplexity. It might be true! How terrifying! The prison door was opening, and the prisoners were too frightened to leave the prison. But it is still true that when theologians of the Roman Catholic Church in the course of independent conversations about the eucharist held in at least three different places at about the same period move away from the theology of the late Middle Ages and of the Counter-Reformation and consciously return to doctrine based upon the New Testament and the early centuries of the Church, the Anglican objective is being fulfilled. The Anglican attitude has made its point. The Anglican protest, if protest it was, has been heard. This does not mean, and this should not mean, that all that remains now is that all Roman Catholics should become Anglicans. It does mean that there is now found to be no insuperable barrier between the Anglican communion and the Roman Catholic communion. No further point now remains in being Anglican for the sake of being Anglican. Anglicanism is not simply (thank God!) the Church of England, though the Church of England is (thank God!) at the heart of Anglicanism. Anglicanism is not just the English way of doing things. It is a serious attempt to work out a Western Reformed Catholicism, and when its theologians and leaders see it travelling along a road which is apparently in the distance to converge with the other Western Catholicism, they should be filled with joy, not pusillanimity. Anglicans should have the courage of their convictions. And the courage of their convictions should carry them steadily towards a full understanding with the Church of Rome, an understanding based, not on cowardly compromise nor servile imitation, but a clear-eyed knowledge that they have reached agreement about the basic truths of the Christian faith. *Modern Eucharistic Agreement* is a landmark on this road.

But none of this will happen, and the bright prospects held out to us by this book will necessarily fade, if the Anglican Communion in general and the Church of England in particular does not show more serious concern for theology. The educational standards of the clergy in the Church of England at least are inexorably declining. The educational standards of the laity are steadily rising. Theology, Christian doctrine, concern for Christian truth, stands in low esteem generally throughout the Church. The kind of excitement and liveliness visible in the newly ordained (who can be taken as representative of the educated younger generation) is not excitement about theological concerns. What apparently moves them is social action and what seems to a person as old as I am to be a vague desire to practise group dynamics on as many people as possible. The intercommunion at local level which is now so freely in operation all over the Church of England arises from no theological imperative and issues in no theological understanding. The theological colleges are in a state of apparently permanent crisis. But there is no substitute for theology, for *logos* about *theos*, for consistent, responsible, heart-searching thought about the significance, the truth, and the claims of the Christian faith. If means can be found to induce Anglicans to pay more attention to theology, to ask themselves more often whether the Christian faith, and their version of it, is true, then the prospect for ecumenical understanding is indeed fair. But before this happens, many obsolete doctrinaire attitudes will have to be abandoned, many hearts and consciences will have to be searched. The kind of atavistic harking-back to lines of fortification long since outflanked by the march of theology which characterized the discussion of the Anglican-Methodist unity scheme must be exorcised. Anglicanism has a rich inheritance waiting for it in the future, but only if it will prove itself worthy of that inheritance.

THE AGREED
STATEMENTS AND THE
EUCHARISTIC TRADITIONS
OF THE CHURCH

Graham Leonard

Three elements constitute the eucharistic tradition of any particular Christian church or communion. Firstly, there is the doctrinal content of the official formularies of the church in question which bear upon the eucharist. Secondly, there is the liturgy which is authorized for use. Thirdly, there is the cult-pattern which is to be found in liturgical practice and which embodies the understanding of the eucharist in local congregations. Each of these three elements has to be taken into account if genuine and long-standing agreement on eucharistic doctrine is to be established between churches.

The doctrinal content of the official formularies bearing upon the eucharist is not to be restricted to specifically eucharistic statements nor to statements about sacraments in general. The sacramental theology of a church can only be accurately determined against the background of its general theological standpoint. In particular the doctrines of creation, redemption, the work of the Holy Spirit, and of eschatology have a special and direct bearing upon its understanding of the eucharist.

The extent to which doctrine is apprehended by members of the Church, and expressed in their lives is, to a very large extent, determined by the form of liturgy which is used in worship and by the manner of its presentation. Few of the laity have any acquaintance with doctrinal formularies, with the possible exception of catechetical documents. The doctrinal content of any liturgy is of great importance because it represents the formal response of a church to the gospel as understood by that church and as expressed in its formularies. Nevertheless any liturgy must of necessity be selective. It is neither intended to be nor can be a manual of Christian doctrine. As is evident from some of the Reformation liturgies, attempts to make the liturgy primarily a means of edification and a safeguard of sound doctrine are self-defeating and result in the conversion of worship into an exercise which is regarded in terms of its benefit to the participant. On the other hand, the basic acts of the liturgy, namely, offertory, consecration, fraction, and communion, are not self-explanatory. Some expression of their significance in verbal form is essential. The prime purpose of the liturgy is to enable the people of God to perform the central act of its life, which is both a duty and a privilege and so be brought into a deeper love of God and obedience to his will in Christ. By its liturgical response to the creative, redeeming, and sanctifying acts of God it learns what it is to be the body of Christ and so to glorify God and fulfil its mission to the world. Christian behaviour is derivative from and dependent upon what God has done and does in Christ. For this reason the liturgy has first to be the proclamation of the divine love and mercy as revealed in Christ and embodied in the life of the Church. As the worshipper is enabled to respond to that proclamation in adoration and obedience, he is truly edified.

While the liturgy must be selective in its doctrinal content, it must be compatible with the official formularies if an inner contradiction and a lack of integrity are not to lie at the heart of the church life. That is not to say that the content of the liturgy must always be subservient to the official formularies. New liturgical understanding may reveal the fact that the formularies embody a distorted or unbalanced sacramental understanding, or because of the time of their origin, may be too dependent upon a particular philosophy of pattern of social thought. In that event it will be the formularies which need modification, not the liturgy. Care, of course, has to be taken that the revised form of liturgy itself does not reflect in an unhealthy way contemporary ideas which are not consonant with the gospel or which result in an unbalanced expression of the gospel.

The relationship between doctrine and liturgy is delicate and complicated. What matters is that the criterion adopted for assessing both is right. The traditional criterion of the Church of England is conformity to holy Scripture and the primitive Church, and as an Anglican I accept that criterion. It does, however, need to be elaborated somewhat. As far as holy Scripture is concerned, the important word is conformity. To seek to base either a liturgical rite or a doctrinal formulary on explicit directions of Scripture and to refuse to embody any element for which there is no direct warrant, is to misunderstand Scripture and to use it in the wrong way. Conformity to holy Scripture should mean that, as the Church living by the Spirit seeks to understand its apprehension of the Christian revelation, or to embody it in its liturgy, nothing is included which is contrary to the nature of God and his dealings with the world as revealed in holy Scripture as a whole.

As far as conformity to the primitive Church is concerned, the same criterion of judgement by the whole of Scripture must be applied. At the same time it must not be assumed that all development in the primitive period is wrong. The elaboration of a very simple eucharistic phrase, for example, may possibly be, for some transitory reason, a reflection of a current social practice. As such it may well be right to discard it and return to the more primitive phrase. It may, on the other hand, have been expressly included to counteract an undesirable or even heretical interpretation of the original phrase. If such an interpretation is likely to occur at the present time, it will probably be most unwise to discard the developed phrase. In other words an appeal to the primitive Church must include an assessment as to which elaborations or enrichments are of permanent value, or at least, of value in the contemporary situation, and which are consonant with holy Scripture.

It follows from what has been said above that in considering modern eucharistic agreements, they cannot be considered simply as documents in their own right and in isolation from the formularies and liturgical practice of the churches to which those who have prepared them belong; to this point we shall return.

The third element in the eucharistic tradition of a church is the cult-pattern. This element is of the greatest importance in considering not only eucharistic agreements but also the ecumenical action which may follow from their production. If visible organic union between the various churches is to be achieved, it must be reflected in the relationships between local Christian congregations. If, in spite of formal eucharistic agreement, the cult-pattern is so diverse that members of the churches concerned cannot express their understanding of that agreement in common eucharistic worship, the local congregation will remain distinct at the very point at which unity really matters. Such inability can stem either from an extreme diversity of rite or from the eucharistic practice of the churches concerned. Diversity of rite may not appear to be a practical problem. An Anglican priest who will have studied liturgy in his training can follow the Orthodox liturgy, different as it is from the rite to which he is accustomed. For the average Anglican layman, however, it would be a very different matter. It may be argued that he is seldom in a position where participation in an Orthodox liturgy is a real issue. That may be so at present, but many Anglicans already travel in Orthodox countries. If eucharistic Agreement is to be implemented effectively in common eucharistic worship, it should mean the end of the situation in which an Anglican abroad seeks an Anglican Church, and if there is not one within reach, does not take his part in the celebration of the liturgy on that particular Sunday.

Nevertheless more acute difficulties arise from a diversity of eucharistic practice, particularly where the Protestant churches are concerned. Frequency of celebration is clearly one issue on which there is diverse practice, though it must not be assumed that the greater the frequency, the greater the importance given to the eucharist in the life of the Church. The frequency of the eucharist with regard both to its celebration and the reception of holy communion has never been as great in the Eastern Church as in the West. Yet no one would for a moment question the absolute centrality of the eucharist in the life of the Orthodox Church. In any case, a distinction must be made between frequency of celebration and the effective place of the eucharist in the mind of the congregation. The eucharist may be celebrated each week at early hour in an English parish church, but the majority of the congregation may only attend Morning or Evening Prayer and apparently be largely unaware of the basic truths set out in a eucharistic agreement. In the Free Churches in England the eucharist, by and large, plays a small part in the thinking of the congregation and is celebrated with relative infrequency. Comparative infrequency of celebration in the Church of Scotland, however, is traditionally associated with a high regard for the sacrament. In some areas the relationship between the eucharist and unity is blurred because of the habit of attending the Free Church for non-sacramental services and the local Anglican Parish Church for Communion. In England generally the growing practice of making the eucharist central to the life of the Church, and, for example, having institutions of new incumbents in the context of the eucharist though many non-communicants may be present, raises the question of eucharistic discipline and the relationship between communion and committed church membership.

The book *Modern Eucharistic Agreement* includes four documents. Two, the Anglican-Roman Catholic Statement and the Lutheran-Roman Catholic Statement, are the product of discussions between representatives of the churches. One, that of the Group of Les Dombes, is the product of an informal group. One is produced by the Faith and Order Commission of the World Council of Churches. The status of each of the documents in relation to the eucharistic tradition of the various churches represented or involved thus differs considerably. The World Council of Churches, for example, not being a church, has no liturgy. The Statement of the Faith and Order Commission cannot be related to the liturgy of the church represented in the same way as should be done in the case of the Anglican-Roman Catholic *Agreed Statement*.

One of the statements, that of the Anglican-Roman Catholic Commission, is strictly doctrinal. The Les Dombes Group has produced two documents, one doctrinal and one pastoral. The Lutheran-Roman Catholic Agreement, though primarily doctrinal, refers to a number of pastoral issues such as communion in both kinds and the communion of the sick. The Faith and Order Commission Statement, while primarily doctrinal, refers in passing to

41

certain practical complications such as the taking of communion to the sick and the nature of the ministry.

None of these could be said to have related their statements realistically to the doctrinal formularies of the churches involved. None of them refer to the liturgies in which the participants express their beliefs in the continuing life of the churches concerned. While some refer to pastoral implications, they do not indicate whether such implications are put into effect in the churches in question or whether they could be if they are not.

If the statements are to be ecumenically effective and are to acquire a greater realism in relation to the life of the churches, it is imperative that they should be examined: *a*. by theologians in relation to the official formularies; *b*. by theologians and liturgists in relation to the liturgies of the churches concerned; *c*. by theologians and by lay people in relation to the cult-pattern, that is, to the actual eucharistic practice in local churches. If these steps are not taken, theological levity will result. Liturgical reform will be be unrelated to the eucharistic agreement which has been reached, and the statements will remain interesting documents which are not reflected in the eucharistic life of the churches.

In the second half of this chapter, I propose to try to give some indications of the kind of questions which must be investigated in respect of the Anglican-Roman Catholic *Agreed Statement* and to do so under the headings of the three elements comprising eucharistic tradition.

1

THE RELATIONSHIP BETWEEN THE AGREED STATEMENT AND DOCTRINAL FORMULARIES

No reference is made to the formularies either of the Anglican Communion or the Roman Catholic Church. In paragraph 1 it is stated that the intention of the Commission has been to 'seek a deeper understanding of the reality of the eucharist which is consonant with biblical teaching and with the tradition of our common inheritance', but it is not clear what is meant by the latter phrase. Is it an oblique reference to the traditional Anglican appeal to the teaching of the ancient Fathers? The weakness arising from the failure to give any content to the phrase 'the tradition of our common inheritance' is well demonstrated by the pamphlet *Christ's Presence and Sacrifice*, by R. T. Beckwith (The Church Book Room Press Ltd., 1973). Mr Beckwith draws attention to the fact that the Commission gives no clear account of the sources on which it draws. He quotes Bishop Butler's article in *The Tablet* which interpreted the tradition of our common inheritance as 'pre-Reformation teaching' and which affirmed that the Commission set aside the decrees of Trent and the Thirty-nine Articles for the time being. This is a somewhat puzzling description of the approach adopted by the Commision, for the statement does not read like a pre-Reformation document. It reads more like a statement of eucharistic theology in the light of the truths rediscovered through the Liturgical Movement in England and on the Continent and in the light of Vatican II, which itself purported to go behind medieval tradition. Perhaps by pre-Reformation tradition Bishop Butler meant the tradition of the patristic period? Or is the phrase 'tradition of our common inheritance' to be qualified by the former phrase 'consonant with biblical teaching', the whole phrase therefore meaning 'such pre-Reformation teaching as is consonant with biblical teaching'? However, the practical effect of the weakness is that Mr Beckwith criticizes the statement on the basis of the decrees of Trent and of the 1662 Prayer Book and the Thirty-nine Articles. In other words we are taken back into the controversies of the sixteenth century and, it might be added, in a way which to a large extent ignores recent changes in Roman Catholic practice. To imply, as Mr Beckwith does, that the Roman Catholic Church disparages the ministry of the Word at a time when it is virtually impossible to attend a Roman Catholic mass at which a sermon is not preached, is quite unrealistic. Some observers of the Roman Catholic scene would question whether the ministry of the Word has not been developed to such an extent that the ministry of the Sacrament is in danger of being disparaged.

If the Commission had said that it put out the *Agreed*

Statement as expressing what is believed to be true, and that the decrees of Trent and the Thirty-nine Articles would have to be examined in the light of it, then the statement itself would have had to be considered on its own merits.

The pamphlet to which reference has already been made also serves to illustrate the need for a specifically eucharistic statement to be set against the background of wide doctrines. Paragraph 3 of the *Agreed Statement* assumes a common understanding of the word 'sacramental' which it is clear that Mr Beckwith does not share. The differences revealed in his pamphlet can, however, only be resolved by a consideration of: *a*. the doctrine of creation and of the relationship of the material world and of those who in flesh and blood live in it, to the Lord who made it; *b*. the relationship between the sacraments as covenanted means of grace and justification by faith. Such an examination would take account of Anglicans who give the impression, however wrongly, of being dualists or nominalists; and of Roman Catholics who give the impression, however wrongly, of being materialists.

2

THE
LITURGIES

Examination of the *Agreed Statement* in relation to the liturgies authorized for use in both churches will be a considerable undertaking, even if it is confined to the Church of England, with four rites now authorized in the Church of England and four eucharistic prayers in the Roman Catholic rite. To carry out such an operation in terms of the Anglican Communion and of the other rites in communion with Rome would indeed be formidable. I shall confine myself to a very brief consideration of the bearing of the liturgies upon what the statement says about the sacrifice of Christ and the oblation.

Section II deals with the eucharist and the sacrifice of Christ. It begins with a fine affirmation of the unique nature of Calvary as the sacrifice by which man is redeemed and reconciled to God. The eucharist is given, by God, so the Statement runs, 'as a means

44

through which the atoning work of Christ on the cross is proclaimed and made effective in the life of the Church'. The remainder of the section deals with the notion of memorial:

The eucharistic memorial is 'no mere calling to mind of a past event or of its significance' but the Church's effectual proclamation of God's mighty acts. Christ instituted the eucharist as a memorial (*anamnesis*) of the totality of God's reconciling action in him. In the eucharistic prayer the Church continues to make a perpetual memorial of Christ's death, and his members, united with God and one another, give thanks for all his mercies, entreat the benefits of his passion on behalf of the whole Church, participate in these benefits, and enter into the movement of his self-offering (*M.E.A.*, pp. 27–8).

It may be noted in passing that there is not a single word in this section to indicate that the memorial is effected in a sacramental way. Except for the reference to the fact that the eucharist was instituted by Christ, the section could be descriptive of the proclamation of God's reconciling acts by the ministry of the Word. The effectiveness of the proclamation in the eucharist is made to depend upon a particular understanding of the notion of memorial in a eucharistic context. This in turn is made to depend upon a particular interpretation of the word *anamnesis*. Mr Beckwith, in his pamphlet referred to above, says quite categorically:

This is contrary both to the etymology and to the usage of the Greek word; and the idea (expressed in the *Agreed Statement*) that this is how the passover 'memorial' was understood in the first century is simply a fashionable fancy, without any historical basis.

Whether his strong words are justified or not, it is clear that the meaning of the word is disputed. It does seem extraordinary to base the central idea of the eucharist, concerning the manner in which the Church is enabled to participate in and benefit from the Lord's saving acts, upon the debatable meaning of one word instead of discussing the nature of the unique mode of sacramental signification. This serves to underline the necessity, referred to above, for the *Agreed Statement* to be examined in the light of the doctrine of creation and of sacramental theology.

The first question which comes to mind on reading the section is 'To whom is the proclamation or the memorial made? Is it to the Church, the world, or God?' The statement gives no answer though the general tenor of the section would imply either a kind of impersonal proclamation for all who have ears to hear, or a proclamation for the benefit of the worshippers. It would not be altogether surprising if it were intended to be understood as the former. Some modern liturgical usage has a strangely impersonal ring and conveys a notion of efficacy which at times appears a parody of the traditional doctrine of *ex opere operato*. Celebration, without particular reference to anybody, as an end in itself, seems to be advocated as a cathartic act. The ideas of adoration of the Father and of the moral obligation laid upon the participants seem strangely muted. In either respect it contrasts sharply with the Lutheran-Roman Catholic statement which says clearly the worshippers 'become participants in his [Christ's] worship, his self-offering, his sacrifice to the Father'. The Les Dombes statement is even more explicit, saying that 'making the memorial of the passion, resurrection, and ascension of Christ our High Priest and Mediator, the Church presents to the Father the one perfect sacrifice of his Son and asks him to accord every man the benefit of the great work of redemption it proclaims'.

When we look at the Anglican and Roman Catholic liturgies, we find that whatever may be the relationship between the offering of the bread and cup and the memorial or proclamation, the latter is made in the context of a prayer to the Father and is directed towards him. So even in the 1662 rite we pray that:

by the merits and death of thy Son Jesus Christ, and through faith in his blood, we and all thy whole Church may obtain remission of our sins, and all other benefits of his passion.

Series III is more explicit:

We celebrate and proclaim his perfect sacrifice . . . accept through him our Great High Priest this our sacrifice of thanks and praise.

Eucharistic Prayer I of the Roman rite says:

> Father, we celebrate the memory of Christ, your Son, we, your
> people and your ministers recall his passion, his resurrection
> from the dead and his ascension into glory and from the many
> gifts you have given to us we offer to you, God of glory and
> majesty, this holy and perfect sacrifice.

In other words, the mediatorial aspect of the work of our Lord,
expressed in Romans 8. 34, 1 John 2. 1, 1 Timothy 2. 5 and
Hebrews 12. 24, is embodied in the liturgies in a way which is not
found in the Statement.

This fact highlights a feature of Eucharistic Prayer III in the
Roman rite. The Statement is strangely silent on the mediatorial
aspect, whereas that prayer presents it in a way which I think is
not to be found elsewhere in Christian liturgies. The *anamnesis*
contains the following words: 'Look with favour on your Church's
offering and see the victim whose death has reconciled us to yourself'. The Latin original is even more stark:

> Respice, quaesumus, in oblationem Ecclesiae tuae agnoscens
> Hostiam cuius voluisti immolatione placari.

It is difficult to see how this agrees with the *Agreed Statement's*
words that Christ instituted the eucharist as a memorial (*anamnesis*) of the totality of God's reconciling action in him. In the
Agreed Statement there is a weak reference to the mediatorial
aspect of the work of the Son but one which does preserve the
Unity of the Godhead. Eucharistic Prayer III would appear to
set the Father over against the Son in an unbiblical way. Had it
been phrased—'and see the victim by whose death you willed to
reconcile the world to yourself', the unity of Father and Son
would have been preserved as in Eucharistic Prayer IV, where the
reference is to 'the sacrifice which you have given to your Church'.
(Note: A similar phrase in the Mozarabic Liturgy to that in
Eucharistic Prayer III is not open to the same objection. Though
it refers to the 'only victim which could appease God', it continues 'since it itself is God', thereby preserving the Unity of
the Godhead in the mediatorial work of Christ.) If agreement is
to be reached on the manner in which the mediatorial work of

Christ is to be manifested sacramentally in the Church, it is essential that agreement be first reached on the nature of the mediatorial work itself.

3
THE CULT-PATTERN

From the point of view of the ordinary worshipper, the cult-pattern is perhaps the most significant of the three constituent elements of the eucharistic tradition. In the first place, the manner in which the eucharist is celebrated, whatever the words of the rite, inevitably conveys a particular understanding of its nature. The celebration of a rite with modern language, such as Series III in the Church of England, in a domestic setting, with very simple vessels and vestments, emphasizes different aspects of eucharistic truth from those which are emphasized if it is celebrated with music, well sung, and with dignified ceremonial in a large parish church of traditional design.

The emphasis given by those taking distinctive parts, particularly the celebrant, which stems from their own understanding and approach, also communicates a certain interpretation of the rite. When it is remembered how seldom the average worshipper takes part in the eucharist other than in his own parish church, the significance of this effect is seen to be considerable.

The cult-pattern has many constituent elements. Reference has already been made to the frequency of celebration and the importance which it is given in the liturgical life of the churches. Other elements include the design of the church building and the emphasis which it conveys; hymns; the vesture of those taking a public part; and the use of a common cup or individual glasses.

Secondly, the cult-pattern to which the ordinary worshipper is accustomed probably represents the most conservative element in his own eucharistic experience and that which is most resistant to change. Many parish priests have found that a parochial church council will agree to adopt a new rite, but will object strongly to changes in ceremonial and setting, however carefully it is pointed out that the rite really demands such changes.

For these reasons it is essential that if a form of eucharistic agreement is to be expressed in the life of the churches which have produced it, it must be embodied in an appropriate cult-pattern. By 'appropriate' is meant, not a single cult-pattern, but one for each Church, which will convey those truths in the statement, or aspects of it, which need to be emphasized in the Church in question. The cult-pattern of the Church of England since the Reformation has built up round the understanding that, whatever else the eucharist may be, it is pre-eminently a communion. Further, in spite of Cranmer's efforts to the contrary, it is understood as an individual matter, though the effect of the parish communion may have modified this somewhat. The cult-pattern of the Roman Catholic Church on the other hand, has, since the early Middle Ages, been built up round the understanding that, whatever else the eucharist may be, it is pre-eminently the offering of a sacrifice. The cult-pattern needed in the Church of England at the present day to recover a fuller understanding of the eucharist is not, therefore, the same cult-pattern which is required by the Roman Catholic Church. It is for this reason, unfortunately, that modern changes in the Roman Catholic cult-pattern have been dominant in the Church of England in recent years, not least in those quarters where it would have been least expected. The Church of England Liturgical Commission, for example, which seems to have gone out of its way *not* to follow the Roman Catholic Church in such matters as the lectionary or the provision of psalmody for the Divine Office (where an ecumenical approach could well be adopted), reflects present Roman Catholic practice very largely in the advice which it gives about the setting and celebration of the revised rites for the eucharist. One criticism which must be made of the Anglican-Roman Catholic *Agreed Statement* is that it does not take sufficient account of the fact that the starting-points of the two churches are different. It is easy to see the relationship between the *Agreed Statement* and the eucharistic teaching in the decrees of Vatican II. It is much more difficult to see the relationship it has to the liturgical debates in the General Synod; yet these reflect in a realistic, if at times regrettable, way the general liturgical understanding of the Church of England. References to necessary changes of emphasis, which should be embodied in changes in liturgical practice, would have made the *Agreed Statement* a more realistic document and one which would probably prove more fruitful.

The production of the various statements calls for nothing less than thanksgiving, but much work now needs to be done if they are to be related effectively to the eucharistic traditions of the churches involved.

EUCHARISTIC AGREEMENT?

Philip Edgcumbe Hughes

If there is one place where Christians should be united it is at the Lord's table, which from the first was intended to be the focus of fellowship, not a denominational barrier. The uncomfortable fact is that, contrary to its purpose, the eucharist has been perverted into an instrument of alienation. This is nowhere more starkly apparent than at, of all places, ecumenical gatherings, such as those of the World Council of Churches, where, devotion to the cult of unity notwithstanding, a common eucharist has been dismissed as impracticable and, instead of being the starting-point, has succumbed to the sophistry which rationalizes it as the idealistic goal towards which the churches must move with caution. As Keith Bridston ruefully declared in 1962, 'In the Ecumenical Movement the sacrament of unity has become more obviously than ever before the sign of disunity' (*Many Churches, One Table, One Church*, WCC, Geneva, 1962, p. 62). Understandably, the younger generation has shown impatience and frustration at the procrastination of their elders and has seen through the shallow device of non-communicating attendance for the purpose of 'spiritual intercommunion', which ignores the dominical command that *all* should eat and drink in remembrance of him. This dissatisfaction led to the 'revolt' at Lausanne in 1960, when members of the Ecumenical Youth Assembly took matters into their own hands and organized a corporate celebration of the sacrament. Evangelicals may justifiably point to the Keswick Convention held annually in England, at which the great corporate communion is a regular and proper feature, gathered as the large assembly is under the banner, 'All One in Christ Jesus'.

Eucharistic oneness is not something which can be imposed 'from above', by superior authority or bureaucratic sanction and organization. It is, and must be, the spontaneous and joyful expression of fellowship in Christ and of the freedom which flows from performing what he has commanded for our blessing. Where there is true unity in Christ and in the grace of the gospel, there is also and for that reason occasion for uniting in the fellowship of his table. Official directives cannot induce that harmony of mind and action which is the effect of the inward operation of the free Spirit of God. Yet it is a harmony that should be sought and cultivated, earnestly and prayerfully. Faith should always seek understanding, and not least where there is a desire to do what our Lord has enjoined.

The first essential in seeking a common understanding is that we should go back together to the New Testament as the dominical fountainhead of our Christian faith and practice. As we do this, the first thing that strikes us is the profound simplicity of the institution of the Supper and of the eucharistic practice of the apostolic Church. What could be simpler than the brief declaration of St Paul to the Christians in Corinth?

> For I received from the Lord what I also delivered to you, that the Lord Jesus on the night when he was betrayed took bread, and when he had given thanks, he broke it, and said, 'This is my body which is for you. Do this in remembrance of me'. In the same way also the cup, after supper, saying, 'This cup is the new covenant in my blood. Do this, as often as you drink it, in remembrance of me'. For as often as you eat this bread and drink the cup, you proclaim the Lord's death until he comes (1 Cor. 11. 23–6, RSV).

No doubt, the significance of the broken bread and the out-poured wine has to be explained in the light of the teaching of the New Testament as a whole concerning Christ's offering up of himself for sinful men, and the sacrament has to be assigned an appropriate position and performance in the liturgical life of the Church; but history shows how rapidly ecclesiastical organization tends to make what is simple elaborate and to impose rigidity where before there was flexibility. In every generation, and not least in ours, there is the need to disencumber the Church of those secondary accumulations which occlude the spirit of apostolic Christianity and to recapture the joyful simplicity of the New Testament. For us today this may well mean breaking out of ecclesiastical structures and restrictions so that, like the earliest believers, we may devote ourselves more genuinely to 'the apostles' teaching and fellowship, to the breaking of bread, and the prayers'—including the breaking of bread hospitably in our homes (Acts 2. 42, 46). We need to see the sacrament not so much as a form to observe, but rather as a privilege to enjoy and a means of grace whereby our oneness in Christ is nourished and lovingly expressed.

Eucharistic teaching may not be systematically presented and developed in the New Testament, but one thing is so obvious as to be universally acknowledged, namely, that this sacrament which our Lord instituted is a *sacrament of the gospel*. It takes us to the very heart of the gospel and it is designed to keep the gospel at the very heart of the life of the Church. Indeed, apart from the gospel of the saving grace of God in Christ Jesus, who procured our everlasting redemption by his atoning death on the cross, where, as he suffered 'the righteous for the unrighteous' (1 Pet. 3. 18), his body was broken and his blood shed (of which the sacramental bread and wine are dramatic symbols), the sacrament is deprived of all meaning; in fact, it ceases to be a sacrament. As preaching should proclaim the gospel audibly, so the eucharist should proclaim the gospel visibly. One of the worst errors in the history of the Church is to imagine that the ministry of the sacrament is something distinct from and other than the ministry of the word. Divorced from the word of the gospel, the sacrament degenerates into superstition. The eucharist belongs to the ministry of the word no less than does preaching. There must be a union of word and sacrament, and no man should put them asunder. Thus the sacrament, as well as the sermon, should preach the gospel to us.

This is simply to say that we need to recover the Augustinian concept of a sacrament as a *visible word*. 'It is when the word is added to the element', says Augustine, 'that the sacrament results, as if itself also a kind of visible word' (*Tractate* 80 on the Gospel of John). Accordingly St Paul speaks of baptism as cleansing 'by the washing of water in the sphere of the word '(Eph. 5. 26). The

53

central focus of the eucharist on the message of the gospel is apparent at the institution of the sacrament, when Christ says, 'This is my body which is *for you*' (1 Cor. 11. 24), and 'This is my blood of the covenant which is poured out *for many*' (Mark 14. 24). In this way the evangelical significance of the sacrament is determined by Christ himself from the very beginning. Not only, then, should the message of the gospel of Christ crucified be proclaimed from the pulpit when the congregation assembles to celebrate the eucharist, but it should interpenetrate the liturgy in its entirety. In the order of holy communion in the Book of Common Prayer, for example, the 'Comfortable Words' are central both in position and in importance, precisely because they are *gospel words*, which, in conjunction with the elements, effect the sacrament for those who draw near with faith. (The four 'comfortable words' are as follows: Matt. 11. 28, 'Come unto me all that travail and are heavy laden, and I will refresh you'; John 3. 16, 'So God loved the world, that he gave his only-begotten Son, to the end that all that believe in him should not perish, but have everlasting life'; 1 Tim. 1. 15, 'This is a true saying, and worthy of all men to be received, that Christ Jesus came into the world to save sinners'; and 1 John 2. 1, 'If any man sin, we have an advocate with the Father, Jesus Christ the righteous, and he is the propitiation for our sins'.) In the 'prayer of Consecration' the recital of the institution is introduced by a plain and forceful declaration of the word of the gospel:

Almighty God, our heavenly Father, who of thy tender mercy didst give thine only Son Jesus Christ to suffer death upon the cross for our redemption; who made there (by his one oblation of himself offered) a full, perfect, and sufficient sacrifice, oblation, and satisfaction, for the sins of the whole world; and did institute, and in his holy Gospel command us to continue, a perpetual memory of that his precious death, until his coming again. . . .

And the administration of the sacrament is also performed within the sphere of the word of the Gospel and the response of faith to that word:

Take and eat this in remembrance that Christ died for thee, and feed on him in thy heart by faith with thanksgiving; 'drink this in remembrance that Christ's blood was shed for thee, and be thankful.

It is thus, by the alliance of word and element, that the gospel becomes visible in the sacrament and that the sacrament becomes a means of grace.

Yet the sacrament is not always and inevitably a means of grace, for the gospel is a sword with two edges. It is indeed true that Christ did not come into the world to judge but to save and that the Gospel is a message of forgiveness and life, not of condemnation and death; but confrontation with the grace of God in Christ Jesus at the same time brings man face to face with the solemn possibility of turning his back on that grace and choosing for himself death instead of life. To love darkness rather than light is to place oneself under judgement, so that the word spoken for man's salvation becomes, if rejected, the word by which man is judged (John 3. 16–21; 12. 46–8). By the same principle, to partake of the sacrament of the eucharist in an unworthy manner, that is, faithlessly and without thanksgiving, is to be 'guilty of profaning the body and blood of the Lord', and to eat and drink judgement upon oneself, so that what is primarily intended as a means of grace becomes instead a means of condemnation (1 Cor. 11. 27–9). In other words, the sacrament, like the gospel word which it visibly portrays, is never without effect. It is not rendered impotent by the unbelieving abuse of man; for the two-edged sword of God's word ever pierces to the heart, if not as an instrument of grace, then as an instrument of judgement (Heb. 4. 12). This being so, the notion that the sacrament invariably functions, *ex opere operato*, as a means of grace to all who receive it, without respect to the state of heart of the recipient, must be set aside as an erroneous and dangerous misunderstanding because it is actually subversive of the gospel and its demands.

Christ is present, then, to give grace through the eucharist, but also, if necessary, to give judgement. But the question of the *eucharistic presence of Christ* has long been one of the great divisive issues in Christendom. Christ was undeniably present at the institution of the eucharist, but not under the forms of bread and wine, for he was physically present in person with his apostles in the upper room. Accordingly, on that original and therefore definitive occasion he could not have intended the apostles to understand that his presence was somehow located in the bread and the wine. At the ascension his physical presence was removed from the earth, but not without the promise that he would return for his own at the end of the age (cf. John 14. 2–3; Acts 1. 9–11; 1 Thess. 4. 15–17). Indeed, the eucharist was ordained by Christ with a view to the period that would intervene between his first and his second comings, a period during which he would be physically and visibly absent. Hence his command, 'Do this in remembrance of me'. A person who is absent is remembered, not one who is present. Hence, too, the apostle Paul's instruction that as often as we partake of the sacramental bread and wine we proclaim the Lord's death 'until he comes' (1 Cor. 11. 26). As Bengel has said in a characteristic epigram, 'Hoc mysterium duo tempora extrema conjungit'. Plainly, then, the sacrament belongs to the time of Christ's bodily absence.

Christ, however, continues to be *really present* in and with his Church, in accordance with his promises, such as, 'Where two or three are gathered in my name, there am I in the midst of them' (Matt. 18. 20); 'Lo, I am with you always, to the close of the age' (Matt. 28. 20); and 'I will never fail you nor forsake you' (Heb. 13. 5). The discussion of the real presence of Christ has been obfuscated for centuries by the strange predisposition to identify the real with that which is physical and visible, despite the clear teaching of the New Testament and of Christian experience that the ultimate reality is that of the spiritual. The bodily absence of Christ does not deprive us of his real presence, which is a spiritual presence, and as such a presence more intimate and real than that of a mere physical presence, since it is the presence of the glorified Redeemer dwelling within each loving and faithful heart (cf. John 17. 23, 26). To quote Jeremy Taylor:

When Christ said, 'Me ye have not always', and at another time, 'Lo, I am with you always, to the end of the world', it is necessary that we distinguish the parts of a seeming contradiction. Christ is with us by his Spirit, but Christ is not with us in body; but if his body be here too, then there is no way of substantial, real presence in which those words can be true, 'Me ye have not always' (*Works*, Vol. II, 1853 edn, p. 719).

Taylor explains that 'all that worthily communicate do by faith receive Christ really, effectually, to all the purposes of his passion', whereas 'the wicked receive not Christ, but the bare symbols only, but yet to their hurt, because the offer of Christ is rejected and they pollute the blood of the covenant by using it as an unholy thing' (Ibid., p. 686).

Richard Hooker, judging that any danger was past 'that men should account of this sacrament but only as of a shadow, destitute, empty and void of Christ', believed that there was 'general agreement concerning that which alone is material, namely the *real participation* of Christ and of life in his body and blood *by means of this sacrament*'. He held, further:

The real presence of Christ's most blessed body and blood is not therefore to be sought for in the sacrament, but in the worthy receiver of the sacrament. And with this the very order of our Saviour's words agreeth, first 'take and eat', then 'this is my body which was broken for you'; first 'drink ye all of this', then followeth 'this is my blood of the new testament which is shed for many for the remission of sins'. I see not which way it could be gathered by the words of Christ, when and where the bread is his body or the cup his blood, but only in the very heart and soul of him which receiveth them. As for the sacraments, they really exhibit, but for aught we can gather out of that which is written of them, they are not really nor do really contain in themselves that grace which with them or by them it pleaseth God to bestow' (*Laws of Ecclesiastical Polity*, v, lxvii, 2, 6).

Hooker's position appeals to me as still eminently sane and solid. It is the position I should wish to advocate as a rallying-point for agreement regarding the eucharist and its significance. Unanimity on every issue that is under discussion is more than can be expected, but can we not agree that our Lord and Saviour ordained this sacrament as a means of grace whereby we do indeed ('in our hearts, by faith, with thanksgiving') eat his flesh and drink his blood, and can we not agree to set aside all notions that an actual change is somehow effected in the elements themselves, so that the 'outward and visible sign' becomes confused with the 'inward and spiritual grace' to which it is intended to direct us? And we can all agree, surely, with the affirmation of the Group of Les Dombes that 'the person and work of Christ, which are the whole content of the gospel, are also the living and dynamic core of the eucharist' (*M.E.A.*, p. 70).

While, moreover, each individual is exhorted to partake by faith and with thanksgiving, yet he does not partake in isolation, for the eucharist is an act of *communion*: the Lord's supper is a communion meal. To quote the Group of Les Dombes again:

> The eucharist is the sacramental meal, the new paschal meal of God's people, which Christ, having loved his disciples unto the end, gave them before his death that they might celebrate it in the light of the resurrection until his coming' (Ibid., p. 57).

The eating of the bread and the drinking of the wine are done in remembrance of his atoning death on the cross. By this eating and drinking the believer, in communion with his fellow believers, not only commemorates what took place at Calvary but also partakes of the benefits of that saving event. But I should wish to contest the concept of this commemoration or memorial (*anamnesis*) as involving an act of 're-presentation', in which 'the Church presents to the Father the one perfect sacrifice of his Son' (*M.E.A.*, p. 58); for this concept confuses, again, the sign with the reality to which it points and has the effect of transforming the table of fellowship into an altar of sacrifice. Christ's command was to eat and drink, not to offer or re-present that sacrifice of our Redeemer which was once offered on the cross. The privilege of the Church is to receive from God the grace that flows from that unique self-offering of Christ. To speak of the eucharist as the occasion when we unite the offering of ourselves with the offering of Christ is to obscure the apostolic doctrine that the sacrifice of Christ was offered *apart from us*: it was not offered *with us*, but *for us*. Thus St Paul says: 'God shows his love for us in that while we were yet sinners Christ died for us' (Rom. 5. 8). It is true that we are also exhorted to present ourselves 'as a living sacrifice, holy and acceptable to God' (Rom. 12. 1), but this is the response of our self-dedication in gratitude for the loving forgiveness and newness of life freely bestowed upon us in Christ. His self-sacrifice is unique because it is the source of our eternal redemption; our self-sacrifice is not redemptive but responsive— the expression of our devotion to him and his cause. 'We love', as St John says, 'because he first loved us' (1 John 3. 19).

And the will of God is that we who know the love of God through faith in the name of his Son Jesus Christ should love one another (1 John 3. 23; 4. 10-11). We are called to be a community of love. How disgraceful, then, if we do not freely and unitedly manifest our love, our joy, and our gratitude in the celebration of the eucharist, which is the sacrament of Christian unity! This unity should be symbolized by the one loaf and the one cup of which all partake, as St Paul teaches:

> When we bless 'the cup of blessing', is it not a means of sharing in the blood of Christ? When we break the bread, is it not a means of sharing in the body of Christ? Because there is one loaf, we, many as we are, are one body; for it is one loaf of which we all partake (1 Cor. 10. 16-17, NEB).

Where this symbolism has been lost, through a multiplicity either of individual wafers or of individual cups, it should be restored as an apostolic token of our oneness in Christ and therefore with each other. Moreover, sectarian barriers which exclude fellow-believers from the Lord's table must be torn down.

As was said at the beginning of this chapter, however, eucharistic fellowship cannot be induced or contrived by the bureaucratic fiats of officialdom, which are more likely to smother than to promote it. Such fellowship must come about spontaneously, at the local level of worship. It will be the consequence not of ecumenical reports or of uniformitarian prescriptions, but of simple Christian open-heartedness which displays itself in open-table hospitality: the Lord's table for the Lord's people. This is not to advocate the administration of the sacrament without discrimination, for within the sphere of the local church membership due discipline should always be exercised; but it is to urge that guests who are present as fellow-believers should be cordially and

E

lovingly welcomed to the fellowship of the Lord's table. Moreover, when Christians from different localities meet together in an assembly of fellow-believers, nothing should be more natural than for them to express their unity of faith and spirit in the fellowship of the Lord's table.

I wish, finally, to take a critical look at a particular method or technique designed, with the best of intentions, to reconcile ecclesiastical differences which is now much in favour in ecumenical circles. This is the device of non-definition or of ambiguous definition. Its development may be attributed largely to the recognition of the hard fact of the intractability of deep-seated convictions and firmly held traditions, with the result that, instead of their being dissolved or discarded, it is now expected that they will be retained, however divisive they may have been in the past. This in turn generally requires the devising of formulas or statements which are offensive to none and acceptable to all, and which predictably either sidestep the more contentious issues or are semantically ambivalent, so that they may be interpreted variously in accordance with the presuppositions that each brings. This method of procedure was well illustrated by the careful avoidance on the part of the Anglican-Methodist Unity Commission of any attempt to define what would take place in the proposed Service of Reconciliation with respect to the orders of ministers from the Methodist Church. The commissioners explained that 'individual participants in the Service may be expected to bring to it diverse and opposing views of its significance' and that 'this must be both admitted and accepted'. Pointing out that 'if either a "Catholic" or an "Evangelical" understanding of the Service appears to be taken, even implicitly, as the norm, many at the opposite extreme will feel that their own convictions about priesthood would be compromised if they took part in it', they concluded that 'if the Service is not to be intolerable to some, neither Church must officially define its significance'. It was declared, further, that 'some will believe that the grace of ordination is given also, others that it is not, and many will be perhaps agnostic on this point', but the assurance was added that 'the prayers are so worded as to leave the determination of the issue in God's hands' (*Towards Reconciliation*, The Interim Statement of the Anglican-

Methodist Unity Commission, 1967, p. 15; *Anglican–Methodist Unity*, Report of the Anglican-Methodist Unity Commission: Part 2, The Scheme, 1968, p. 127).

This has every appearance not only of 'passing the buck' to the Almighty but also of setting the official seal of approval on the state of disarray and contradiction now so widely prevalent in the Church, a most unapostolic procedure! We are evidently on the threshold of that state of affairs, satirically predicted by Ronald Knox sixty years ago, in which the Church, 'true to her catholic vocation', will 'include within her borders every possible shade of belief, *Quod umquam, quod usquam, quod ab ullis*'! (*Reunion All Round*, 1914, p. 32).

It was the failure to define what the proposed Service of Reconciliation was intended to effect in terms of ministerial and eucharistic competence that caused the scheme for Anglican-Methodist union to founder. Within the sphere of Anglicanism, the bishops at the Lambeth Conference of 1958 had persuaded themselves, it seems, that 'the time has come to claim that controversies about the eucharistic sacrifice can be laid aside, the tensions surrounding this doctrine transcended'. The ground of this belief was a construction which postulated a concept of eucharistic incorporation of the sacrifice of ourselves into the sacrifice of Christ (on which some comments have been offered above). It was the Roman Catholic theologian Francis Clark who drew attention to the 'significant ambiguity' of the synthesis proposed by the bishops, observing that 'different constructions may be placed upon the language according to different presuppositions' (*Eucharistic Sacrifice and the Reformation*, 1960, p. 520). This criticism applies with even more force to the 1971 Anglican-Roman Catholic statement on the eucharist (*M.E.A.*, pp. 26 ff.), which is a masterpiece of this type of equivocation. I am in complete agreement with the judgement of Francis Clark concerning the inadequacy and ultimate futility of attempting to resolve oppositions in the Church by bringing them together into a specious state of harmony. He writes as follows:

Despite the new spirit of conciliation and the careful choice of terms, it does not appear that the essentials of the problem have been changed. The new comprehensive language ... may cover, but it does not resolve, the basic doctrinal tensions. ... In the long run the ecumenical cause will be better served by frank scrutiny of the roots of disagreement than by ignoring them. The clear-sighted candour of writers like Bishop Neill, who are able to recognize the incompatibility of two doctrinal positions and to point out the reason, is more useful than the well-meant but undiscerning eirenism of writers who treat contradictory doctrines as complementary insights, as different emphases of the same truth, as different colours in one spectrum of Christian witness (Op. cit., p. 522).

To resort to fine-sounding but ambivalent terminology is to paper over the cracks and then to call attention to the attractiveness of the wall-paper. This is no way to strengthen or rebuild the structure of the Church. That there is a better way I have tried to show above.

RECENT THOUGHT
ON THE THEOLOGY OF
THE EUCHARIST

E. L. Mascall

One of the most striking phenomena in the ecumenical field in recent years has been the unexpected measure of agreement that has been achieved by representatives of the various Christian confessions in the realm of eucharistic belief. We are all familiar with the remarkable *Agreed Statement on Eucharistic Doctrine* completed in September 1971 by the Anglican–Roman Catholic International Commission after meetings spread over the previous two years, but there are others, more local in scope but nevertheless impressive, such as those produced in Scotland by Roman Catholics and Anglicans and in the USA by Roman Catholics and Lutherans, and on the European continent by Roman Catholics and Protestants. It would, however, be a mistake to suppose that such agreements are simply the results of negotiations between the various groups whose names they bear; while these latter are by no means to be despised, there lies behind them a whole mass of research and discussion on the plane of pure scholarship which goes back to the early years of this century and is still going on today. It is to a brief account of this that I propose to devote the present essay, and I shall deal in sequence with the eucharistic sacrifice and the eucharistic presence, though the two topics are of course intimately interrelated.

As long ago as 1930 Dr F. C. N. Hicks in his book *The Fulness of Sacrifice* drew attention to the way in which, both during the Reformation and after, discussions of the eucharist had been dominated by the medieval conception of sacrifice as consisting exclusively in the death of the victim, this being taken in complete isolation from the circumstances which led up to it, accompanied it or followed from it. The consequence of this was a situation in which each side had an argument which was quite invulnerable to the attacks of the other. The Protestants were in effect incessantly asserting 'Christ being raised from the dead dieth no more; therefore the eucharist cannot be a sacrifice', while the Catholics as constantly replied 'But the eucharist is a sacrifice, therefore in some sense Christ must be put to death in it'; neither side observed the suppressed major premise which was common to both arguments, namely that sacrifice is simply equivalent to death. For Catholics, therefore, the eucharist was seen as a *repetition* of Calvary, while for Protestants it was at most a *commemoration* of Calvary. In actual fact both parties tended to mitigate the less acceptable aspects of their positions. Catholics have generally asserted that, while the eucharist is a repetition of Calvary, it is not a *literal* repetition, while many Protestants have been anxious to insist that, while it is a commemoration of Calvary, it is not a *bare* commemoration; but what exactly is involved in a repetition which is not literal or a commemoration which is not bare, neither side has found it easy to explain. Many of the great Anglican divines readily describe the eucharist as a sacrifice, but with various qualifying adjectives, which, while their purpose is clearly to rule out literal repetition, are not as a rule easy to interpret.

It is only right to say that this interpretation of the situation has been vigorously and elaborately attacked by Dr Francis Clark in his work *Eucharistic Sacrifice and the Reformation*, but both his selection of material and his interpretation of it have in turn been attacked by Dr John J. Hughes in his own book *Stewards of the Lord*. While he is far from maintaining that the views of the Reformers were invariably sound and Catholic, Hughes argues very convincingly that, by the end of the Middle Ages, not only popular practice and parochial homiletics but also the thought of professional theologians on the subject of the eucharist had become distorted and unbalanced and that Catholic scholars were quite incapable of making an adequate response to the, often justifiable, polemics of the Reformers. Largely, he holds, this was due to the almost complete concentration of medieval eucharistic theology on the question of the sacramental presence of Christ, so that the question of the eucharistic sacrifice was dealt with inadequately and indeed often quite incorrectly. Taking the fifteenth-century nominalist theologian Gabriel Biel as his chief example, Hughes shows that the generally accepted view was that the principal minister of the mass was not Christ but either the celebrating priest or else the Church, considered not in its character as the body and instrument of the ascended Lord but as an earthly organization. In consequence, whereas the sacrifice offered by Christ as God incarnate on Calvary was seen as having an infinite value, the sacrifice offered by a finite celebrant in the mass was seen as having only a limited value. Hence the need to multiply the number of masses in order to obtain a sufficiently large, though still finite, aggregate value, and the existence of a large number of priests whose sole ecclesiastical function was the celebration of mass. The only late medieval theologians holding that the principal celebrant of the mass is Christ, whom Hughes can find, are Cajetan and Kaspar Schatzgeyer, and he comments on the remarkable fact that, in spite of Cajetan's great reputation, his view on this particular and vital question seems to have had no influence at all.

In all this part of his argument Hughes makes full use of the recent work of Hans B. Meyer, Erwin Iserloh, and Notker Halmer. While recognizing Clark's achievement in showing that 'destruction theories' of the eucharistic sacrifice are mainly post- and not pre-Tridentine, he insists on the centrality of the question: what was the view of the eucharistic sacrifice and of priesthood which the Anglican reformers rejected? His reply, given after a detailed examination of their writings and those of their opponents, to which I can make only passing reference here, is that it was a view which no Catholic theologian today would countenance for one moment and which is totally inconsistent with the teaching of Vatican II. It was a view which (while he notes that even Trent used the word 'sacrifice' in no less than thirteen different senses in discussing the mass) Hughes traces down to Cardinal Vaughan and beyond, that the primary essence of the priesthood is the power to change bread and wine into the body and blood of Christ.

With the bearing of this research on the validity of Anglican orders, which is the chief topic of Dr Hughes' book, I am nor concerned here. I will only outline the way in which a deeper understanding of the meaning of the eucharistic sacrifice has been achieved. It is interesting to note that not only theologians but also anthropologists have had a share in this, for it reaches back into the origins of sacrifice as deeply rooted in human religion as such. The chief honour for this is due to the French theologian Eugène Masure, in his book *Le Sacrifice du Chef* (2nd edn, 1932; E.T., *The Christian Sacrifice*), but it received independent confirmation in the book by the American Episcopalian R. K. Yerkes, *Sacrifice in Greek and Roman Religions and Early Judaism* (1952). Both these writers maintain that, while sacrifice can take grisly and horrible forms, the basic meaning of sacrifice is not the destruction of a creature for the glory of God, but the offering of it to God in recognition of him as its creator, in order that it shall be accepted by him and transformed by his acceptance of it. Thus, in being offered to God in sacrifice, the creature is simply fulfilling the law of its being as a creature, for God is both its efficient and its final cause, its alpha and its omega, its beginning and its end. As Hicks made plain from his study of Judaism, the essence of sacrifice is not death but the offering of life. When the victim is a lifeless or irrational object, the sacrifice can hardly be more than figurative and external, for neither the understanding nor the will of the victim can have any part in it. The true sacrifice, the sacrifice that God can accept and transform and that, when transformed, is of value in itself, is the offering by a rational creature of itself. Man, then, created by God and for God, was meant to achieve his fulfilment and beatitude by offering himself to the Father in a life of joyful and loving filial response, which would be an analogous reflection on the created level of the eternal act of filial response made by the Son on the uncreated level in the life of the Trinity; for the Son is the Father's image, and man is made in the image of God. Sin has, however, entered in and man is, in the biblical phrase, at enmity with God; the consequence is that sacrifice becomes extraordinarily deviant and ambiguous. Man, knowing in the depths of his being that he can no longer offer himself to God, finds himself offering other

66

creatures to God instead of himself. The truth that he cannot apprehend but that will one day be revealed to him is that what is needed is not that he should offer other creatures instead of himself, but that someone other than himself should offer him. And this is what happens through the incarnation of the eternal Son.

When the divine Word took flesh in the womb of his Virgin Mother, it was in order that in manhood there should be made that perfect filial offering to the Father that man throughout his history had so signally failed to make. In the hypostatic union the manhood of Jesus is taken up into that act of filial response that the Son ever makes to the Father in the life of the Trinity. Thus, from the moment when the divine Word took flesh in Mary's womb, throughout his earthly life and beyond his ascension to his present glorified condition in heaven, the human life of the divine Son and the human nature in which he lives it are one continuous offering to the Father, continuously accepted and continuously transformed. In the words of Denys the Carthusian, 'the whole life of Christ on earth was, as it were, one solemn Mass, in which he himself was the altar and the temple, the priest and the victim'.

What, then, is the place in this of the cross and the death on Calvary? They are essential and inevitable when a perfect offering of a human life is made in a fallen world. Christ gave himself completely in his whole life; he did not slay himself. But the making of a perfect offering in a sinful world inevitably drew down upon itself the concentrated forces of evil in a desperate attempt to destroy it or to mutilate its perfection. So the life passed through death, in a way of which the death of the victim in the ancient sacrifices was only the faintest and most remote foreshadowing. Nevertheless the death was the offering of the life and not its destruction, and in the resurrection it was accepted by the Father and transformed into a condition of perpetual efficacy. Christ ever liveth to make intercession for us.

But what is the bearing of this on the sacrifice of the eucharist? The offering that the ascended Christ makes of himself to the Father in his glorified manhood is communicated to the Church which is his body by the descent of the Spirit at Pentecost, and to its members, who are his members, by their baptismal incorporation into him. As St Paul told his Roman correspondents, Christian baptism is an actual participation in the death and resurrection of Christ; in the words of the Epistle to the Ephesians God has raised us up and made us to sit with him in the heavenly places in Christ Jesus. So our lost sonship is restored through our incorporation into Christ, we are *filii in Filio*, and the Church, which is Christ's body, is also the family, the household of God.

So it is in the eucharist that the Church is continually sustained and renewed in her character as Christ's body. By the eucharist the Church is made what she already is and Christians are made what they already are. I think it has come to be seen in recent years that the only doctrine of the eucharistic sacrifice that is both adequate and tolerable is one that understands the eucharist as neither a repetition nor a commemoration of the Sacrifice of Christ, but as identically the *same* sacrifice, differing only in the mode of its presentation. This takes us back to Masure.

How can we share in the sacrifice of him who is our head, Masure inquires, the sacrifice which consists in the return of the Son to the Father with his religion of adoring love, accomplished in the hard conditions which our sins imposed? Through our participation in the sacrament of the eucharist, he replies, and this leads him to consider the meaning of *sacrament*. A sacrament, he tells us, is fundamentally a *sign* or *symbol* and the function of a sign is to put before us the reality which it signifies. The mass, therefore, is not a further event which happens to Christ in the historical order, a new episode in his biography. The whole sacrifice is contained and communicated under the sacramental symbols. This, Masure asserts, was the teaching of both St Thomas and the Council of Trent, but it was lost by the post-Reformation theologians, who looked for some element or aspect of the mass which could be recognized as, virtually if not really, a new immolation of Christ. Masure had himself shown some vacillation as to the way in which the mass 'pictures' the death of Christ; he seemed to be somewhat embarrassed by the encyclical *Mediator Dei* of Pope Pius XII in 1947, but on the central point he was clear. 'The sacramental sign', he wrote, 'is not efficacious because it symbolically resembles the mystery to be produced by it. It is efficacious because it has been instituted by our Lord.'[1]

68

On this question of the nature of sacramental signification Masure had in fact been anticipated by Dom Anscar Vonier, whose book *A Key to the Doctrine of the Eucharist* had appeared in 1925, though Vonier himself had been anticipated by R. I. Wilberforce in the middle of the nineteenth century. For Vonier the essence of an effectual sign, such as the eucharist, is that the causality which it exercises is of an entirely unique type. It is a sign which brings about what it signifies and it does this simply because it is a divinely ordained sign of it. It is, of course, supernatural, but not all supernatural causality is sacramental. 'Sacraments are a new creation with entirely new laws. . . . The sacramental world is an unknown world with a well-known inhabitant.'[2] It is true that Vonier tended, in the medieval manner, to identify Christ's sacrifice too exclusively with his death, but that is easily corrected. What is of first importance is his recognition that the mass is not a new episode in the life of Christ which in some way repeats or imitates his death, but is the means by which the whole sacrificial action of Christ is made sacramentally present in the Church. Making the necessary correction we may say that, in the sacramental order, the eucharist contains and communicates the whole saving activity of Christ, the whole sweep of filial self-oblation that extends from his incarnation in the womb of Mary through his death on Calvary to his heavenly glorification. The eucharist is therefore neither a new sacrifice nor a part of the one sacrifice; it *is* the one Sacrifice in its totality, present under and by a divinely ordained efficacious sign.

Earlier than Vonier an attempt had been made by the Jesuit theologian Maurice de la Taille to find an alternative to the repetition view of the eucharist by distinguishing three elements in a sacrifice, namely a ritual oblation, an immolation, and a divine acceptance, and identifying the Eucharist with the ritual element; his great volume *Mysterium Fidei* was completed in 1915. Hicks, in 1930, based a similar view on the fact that in the Old Testament sacrifices the essentially priestly and sacrificial act was not the slaying of the victim, which might be performed by a lay person, but the offering on the altar to God of the blood which was identified with its life. A similar view was developed by the Anglican lay theologian Will Spens in the late 1920s. The strong points of this approach are obvious, but it suffers from the fact that, in making the eucharist an integral part of Christ's sacrifice, it implies that without the eucharist Christ's sacrifice would be incomplete; and this is very difficult to admit.

Space will allow of only brief reference to the work which has been done from the Protestant side by such writers as J. D. Benoît, D. M. Baillie, J. Leenhardt, Geddes MacGregor (now for some years an Anglican), Max Thurian, and Gustaf Aulén. I have discussed them in some detail in my book *Corpus Christi*. Many of them are ready to use sacrificial language in connection with the eucharist, so long as there is no suggestion that Christ's sacrifice is either incomplete without it or is repeated by it. Several of them, and in particular Thurian, commenting on Christ's command at the Last Supper 'Do this as my *anamnesis*', argue that the meaning of *anamnesis* is not a mere psychological act of remembering but a literal bringing into the present of an event or a reality which is chronologically in the past. Such a view, of course, neatly coheres with the view which we have found in some of the Catholic writers, that in the eucharist the whole of Christ's redemptive activity is present by sacramental causality. Two final remarks must be made before we pass on to consider the eucharistic presence. First, there has been a growing recognition that Christ, in instituting the eucharist with the material substances of bread and wine, has manifested a special concern with the physical universe, of which man, in his bodily aspect, is a part. Thus the eucharist is not only the sacramental and eschatological representation of the redeemed community; it is also the sacramental and eschatological representation of the restored and transfigured universe. Pierre Teilhard de Chardin's famous theological rhapsody *The Mass on the World* receives its justification here. Secondly, we can, I think, see an answer to the bitterly argued question 'Who offers what in the eucharist, if indeed anyone offers anything at all?' Does Christ offer Christ, or does Christ offer us, or do we offer Christ, or do we offer ourselves, or do we merely offer bread and wine? Merely to state the question in this way, I suggest, presupposes an artificial and perverse separation between Christ and his members, a morcellation or fragmentation of the body of Christ. If we recognize the Pauline doctrine, on which

Emile Mersch insisted throughout his writings, that the Whole Christ is the Head and his members as one mystical body, through the hypostatic union of the incarnation and the adoptive union of baptism—*Totus Christus membra cum capite. Unum corpus multi sumus*—we shall, I think, be content to say that in the eucharist the Whole Christ offers the Whole Christ and build up any further speculations on that basis.

It can hardly have escaped my readers that almost all the writings to which I have referred are at least a quarter of a century old and that some are much older than that; and indeed apart from some not very successful attempts to utilize the language and concepts of existentialist philosophy there is, I think, little to add as far as the basic theological understanding of the eucharistic sacrifice is concerned. These new—or, it would be better to say, newly recovered—insights have, however, had an enormous impact in the spheres of practical spirituality, pastoral ministry and eucharistic practice. Many of the documents of Vatican II show their influence, and such an admirable book as *His Presence in the World* by Fr Nicholas Lash is typical of a whole mass of writing concerned with the level where systematic theology and the pastoral task converge and interlock. And this is as it should be, for the eucharist is not just a happy hunting ground for theological specialists but the food from which Christ's body and its members derive their supernatural life.

Passing now to the eucharistic presence, the first point to be stressed is that, however convenient it may be to distinguish the sacrifice and the presence in theoretical discussion, neither can be adequately understood without reference to its organic union with the other. The presence is for the sake of the sacrifice, but there could be no sacrifice without the presence. And when one reflects on the violence of the controversy that has raged from the sixteenth century onwards round the word 'transubstantiation', it is significant that in the *Agreed Statement* of the Anglican–Roman Catholic International Commission the word is relegated to a footnote as a term used by Roman Catholics to denote the reality of the eucharistic presence and not as implying of necessity any particular view as to how that presence is brought about or what its metaphysical character is. As regards the objective reality of the presence the Statement shows no wavering, though it keeps the presence firmly in the context of the eucharistic rite and the act of communion.

> The elements are not mere signs; Christ's body and blood become really present and are really given. But they are really present and given in order that, receiving them, believers may be united in communion with Christ the Lord.

And again:

> The bread and wine become the body and blood of Christ by the action of the Holy Spirit, so that in communion we eat the flesh of Christ and drink his blood.

It is thus clear that the Commission believed that it is possible to state the doctrine of the eucharistic presence without committing oneself to any particular metaphysical system, such as Thomist Aristotelianism, and even to use the term 'transubstantiation' without doing so. It must, however, be admitted that very few discussions of the presence seem to have preserved this metaphysical neutrality. To a great extent this seems to arise from a tendency to which most of us are subject when we get involved in philosophizing about Christian truth, namely that, while we are vividly conscious of the weakness and ephemerality of the philosophies of the past, we tend to look upon those to which we ourselves adhere as invulnerable and final. Furthermore we tend to attribute theological authority to conclusions which we have reached by applying the philosophy in question. Thus Charles Gore, while rejecting transubstantiation as 'a verbal incumbrance due to an inopportune intrusion into church doctrine of a temporary phase of metaphysics',[3] based his own doctrine of the eucharistic presence on the quasi-Kantian idealism of his day without any suspicion that that might in turn be only a temporary phase. Will Spens, again, based *his* doctrine of the Eucharistic presence on what he took to be the underlying metaphysics of physical science in the Cambridge of the 1920s; and it is interesting to notice that, while Gore's view led to the consequence that extra-liturgical devotion to the eucharistic elements was unallowable, Spens's view led to the consequence that it was allowable and praiseworthy. Here, more than in most branches of theology, it is difficult to disentangle Christian doctrine from the particular conceptual system in which it happens to be expressed, and it is striking that the encyclical *Mysterium Fidei*, issued by Pope Paul VI in September 1965, while it clearly attempts to remain on the strictly doctrinal level and to avoid being involved in contemporary philosophical issues, is only doubtfully successful in doing this. The Pope was visibly troubled by some of the contemporary attempts to understand the eucharistic change in terms of the notions of 'transfinalization' and 'transignification', and he denounced as intolerable the abandonment or modification of the Tridentine formulations. Nevertheless, he said explicitly that these formulas 'express concepts which are not tied to any specified cultural system'. He said: 'They are not restricted to any fixed development of the sciences or to one or other of the theological schools. . . .

> They present the perception which the human mind acquires from its universal, essential experience of reality and expresses by use of certain terms borrowed from colloquial or literary language. They are therefore within the reach of everyone at all times and in all places. They may indeed [he continued] have a clearer and more obvious exposition, but only with the same meaning as that with which they were employed. This enables the unalterable truth of faith to survive as progress is made in understanding of faith.

Clearly Pope Paul was not offering a solution to the problem indicated by his predecessor in the famous words 'The substance of the ancient doctrine contained in the deposit of faith is one thing; its formulation is quite another'; but no less than Pope John he was concerned to warn against superficial treatments of it.

The writers who introduced the notions of transfinalization and transignification were worried that the term 'transubstantiation' as commonly understood suggested a notion both insufficiently dynamic and insufficiently human. 'Bread' and 'wine', they asserted, denote not merely certain physical objects but those objects as nutritive for man, and so, when they became nutriment for his supernatural as well as his natural end, their meaning (*significatio*) and their purpose (*finis*) have been changed; hence, 'transignification' and 'transfinalization'. And Pope Paul, so far from denying this, expressly asserted it, but he saw it as following from, and amplifying, the concept of transubstantiation and not as supplanting it. 'When transubstantiation has taken place,' he wrote, 'there is no doubt that the species of the bread and the species of the wine take on a new significance and a new finality.' But, he continued, 'They take on a new significance and a new finality for the very reason that they contain a new "reality" which we are right to call *ontological*.' What was condemned, then, was not transignification and transfinalization, but the reduction of transubstantiation to these and nothing more. And the resolution of this doubt will clearly depend on the philosophical context in which the notions of signification and finality are being used.

A similar question arises in connection with William Temple's theory of 'transvaluation', expounded in his book *Christus Veritas* in 1924. For him the ultimate aspect of reality was not *being*, as for a Thomist, but 'value':

> In this book [he wrote] we have seen reason to think that what St Thomas ought to have meant when he said 'substantia' was what we mean when we say 'Value'; though, of course, he did not mean this. If Transubstantiation means Transvaluation the objections to it partly disappear; otherwise they are very formidable.[4]

I am tempted myself to say that if 'transvaluation' means 'transubstantiation' the objections to *it* partly disappear, for they seem to me to be very formidable unless value is identified with substance or being, in accordance with the maxim *Omne ens est unum, verum, bonum*, so that value (*bonum*) is metaphysically a consequence of being (*ens*) and not *vice versa*. However, if you hold that value is the ultimate reality, you can hardly describe a more total change of anything than by saying that its value has changed; and similarly if you hold that the ultimate reality of anything is its signification or its purpose. But the question still remains whether a philosophy which holds value or signification or purpose to be the ultimate reality provides a satisfactory vehicle for the communication of the truths of the Christian religion. This, I think, is what troubled the Pope, and I must confess that it troubles me. For, while there may be more than one philosophy that provide an adequate vehicle, there are certainly some that do not; and this cannot be decided in advance.

The most recent discussion of the eucharistic presence that I have seen is to be found in some articles in *New Blackfriars* by a Roman Catholic writer using the pseudonym G. Egner.[5] He makes an all-out attack on the doctrine of transubstantiation both as it is expounded by St Thomas and also in the briefer and less elaborate formulation of the Council of Trent. He argues, first, that the Aristotelian and Thomist doctrine of change in terms of transition from potentiality to act becomes incoherent when it is applied to *substantial* and not merely to *accidental* change and, secondly, that it becomes even worse when it is applied to the eucharistic transformation, since it can then mean only that Christ is made out of bread. He is, moreover, equally critical of the views which some of the Flemish and Dutch theologians have formulated in opposition to the Thomist and Tridentine treatment, though he thinks that these thinkers have not done quite as much violence to their own philosophy in extending it to the eucharist as St Thomas and Trent did to theirs.

The setting in which these 'new' theologians have cast their thinking is that of the phenomenology associated with the name of Edmund Husserl. Its attractive features are that it thinks in terms of humanity rather than of nature in general, it sees our human corporeal nature essentially in terms of communication, and it sees the world not just as a receptacle in which we find ourselves placed but as constituted by the activity and inter-relations of human beings. It therefore might seem to provide a context for Eucharistic theology which would emphasize the *personal* presence and activity of Christ in the eucharist in contrast with tendencies to think of the consecrated elements as simply very holy *things*. Typical of this view is the assertion that 'Things are purely and simply what they are for Christ, because the mind of Christ is the absolute norm of our own mind, just as his own existence is. Perceptible and physico-chemical properties have only a relative meaning'.[6] Egner's objection is that to talk like this is to fall into what he calls 'the Fallacy of Replacement'; that

75

is to say, it is to substitute a new set of questions and answers for the original set, without noticing that the old set still retain their meaning. Thus, he says, if the consecrated host has all the physical properties of bread, it *is bread*, and no amount of new significance given to it by Christ or anyone else can alter this fact. I must confess that this objection of Egner's does not convince me; it reminds me too much of the way in which the logical positivists defined the meaningfulness of statements as empirical verifiable and then deduced that only empirically verifiable statements were meaningful. The most traditional Thomist will not define substance in terms of simply physical properties, for he will hold that angels are substances (spiritual substances) although they have no physical properties whatever. I am in fact highly sceptical of the validity and the utility for theological purposes of Husserlian phenomenology, as I am of the validity and utility of Heideggerian existentialism, but I am not persuaded of the cogency of Egner's objections. And I am not sure that Egner's rejection of transubstantiation rests upon anything more than the very restricted connotation which he gives to the word 'substance'. On the other hand, the brief outline which he gives of his own approach, and which is to be amplified in a forthcoming book, is highly promising. It starts from the basic human activity of eating, proceeds to the ritual significance of eating in human history as a whole and in the history of Judaism, with its culmination in Christ's actions at the Last Supper as making us to share in his redemptive and liberating act and as showing how his own blood seals the new and everlasting covenant between God and mankind. 'Whatever we say of the eucharistic presence of Christ must be said in the context of the ritual meal.' 'What I assert,' he says, 'differs from the newer theology in its refusal to let the reality of Christ's gift negate the reality of the earthly means of its giving.'[7] This is finely said, but is it in fact fair to the newer theology? If what things are is what they are for Christ, does the new meaning which the elements acquire by consecration destroy the meaning that they had before and not rather include it? Egner legitimately reminds us that grace does not destroy nature but perfects it; am I merely mischievous in suggesting that Egner's own approach might be seen

76

as destroying the older views rather than as perfecting them?

I do not think that we have yet reached even a relatively stable view of the eucharistic presence in the way in which, for example, we may be seen to have reached one as regards the eucharistic sacrifice. I shall devote the space which remains to a few suggestions which may be worth while following up.

Many recent writers have urged the importance of the concept of relationship in theology. I do not think, however, that it is sufficient merely to emphasize the relational character of objects in contrast to their qualities. Relations, no less than qualities, can be static and lifeless; the relations involved in the eucharistic presence must be not static but dynamic. Even this is not enough, however, for dynamic relations can be lifeless and impersonal; the relations of the eucharistic presence must be not merely dynamic but also personal. May I illustrate this by an anecdote. At the Malvern Conference, which was held in the early days of the Second World War, the Chairman, Archbishop William Temple, produced a statement about the eucharist in which it was said that the Church offers bread and wine to God and that God returns them to us 'charged with spiritual power'. Dr Temple's intention was obvious; he was anxious to assert the real efficacy of the sacrament without dividing his audience by making controversial statements about the nature of the eucharistic presence. He was, I think, rather surprised when I suggested to him privately that the wording which he had chosen, and which seemed to rest upon an analogy derived from electrostatics, might easily be taken to imply a view of the eucharistic presence which had no particular relation to the atoning work of Christ, did not necessarily imply a *personal* presence at all, and was redolent of magic and gnosticism, whereas the traditional language firmly rooted the eucharist in the acts performed at a definite historical epoch by the historical personage Jesus of Nazareth. (My point was not in fact taken.) *Dynamis* (power or force), can be purely impersonal, as we see from such words as 'hydrodynamics' and 'electrodynamics'; it is thus not enough to say that the Eucharistic elements are the terms of dynamic relations unless we add that those relations are personal ones. It may still be asked, however, how elements can be the terms of personal relations when all their

77

properties that are perceptible to the senses are those of lifeless objects, namely bread and wine. We must, I suggest, pay attention to the fact that the elements after consecration are described as Christ's 'body' and 'blood'.

In biblical thought, 'flesh' or 'flesh and blood' denotes not a part of human nature, but human nature in its entirety or the human individual as such. To say that the eucharistic element is Christ's body is thus to say that it is the totality of his very self, the man Christ Jesus, the Word incarnate, the subject of his personal dynamic relations to the individual Christian, to the Church, to the human race and to the universe as a whole. Admittedly, we cannot hold a two-way conversation with Christ in the Sacrament. There is, however, a more intimate mode of communion than conversation, namely vital union, and it is this that the eucharist provides. In it Christ is given to us as our food and drink, our nourishment and refreshment, we are made one with him and he with us; but with this great difference from natural eating and drinking, as the fathers so frequently emphasize, that here the food is not assimilated to the recipient, but the recipient is assimilated to the food. There is indeed a transignification, for the elements effectually signify not just the maintenance of the recipient as a member of the early community but his maintenance in the supernatural organism which is Christ's body the Church. There is also a transfinalization, for the elements are directed not simply to the recipient's destiny in his earthly life with its conclusion in bodily death but to his supernatural destiny with its culmination in the resurrection of the body and the beatific vision. And in each case nature is not destroyed or ignored by the supernatural, but is gathered up and perfected by it.

Finally, although Christ's presence in the eucharistic elements is of supreme and central importance, it is not his only presence in the eucharist nor is his presence in the eucharist his only presence in the Church and the world. As the Liturgical Constitution of Vatican II eloquently declared,

Christ is always present in his Church, especially in her liturgical actions. He is present in the sacrifice of the mass, not only in the person of his minister . . . but especially under the eucharistic species. By his power he is present in the sacraments, so that when a man baptizes it is really Christ himself who baptizes. He is present in his word, since it is he himself who speaks when the holy Scriptures are read in church. He is present lastly when the Church prays and sings. . . .

Christ indeed always associates the Church with himself in this great work wherein God is perfectly glorified and men are sanctified. The Church is his beloved Bride, who calls to her Lord and through him offers worship to the Eternal Father.[8]

It is in this context that I believe all our theologizing about the eucharist should be carried on.

NOTES

1. *The Christian Sacrifice*, p. 225n.
2. Op. cit., pp. 35, 92.
3. *The Body of Christ*, p. 120.
4. Op. cit., p. 247.
5. August and September 1972; April 1973. Discussion by E. L. Mascall and H. McCabe, December 1972.
6. Art. cit., September 1972, p. 401.
7. Ibid., p. 405.
8. *Constitution on the Liturgy*, n. 7, amplified by Pope Paul VI, *Mysterium Fidei*, n. 35.